The Social Security Crisis of 2037
(a compelling scientific explanation for the certain
Social Security crisis and how it impacts you)

The Social Security Crisis of 2037

(a compelling scientific explanation for the certain Social Security crisis and how it impacts you)

James LePage Ph.D., CPA (retired)

authorHOUSE®

AuthorHouse™
1663 Liberty Drive
Bloomington, IN 47403
www.authorhouse.com
Phone: 1 (800) 839-8640

Published by AuthorHouse 10/16/2015

ISBN: 978-1-5049-3364-3 (sc)
ISBN: 978-1-5049-3363-6 (hc)
ISBN: 978-1-5049-3428-2 (e)

Library of Congress Control Number: 2015914157

Print information available on the last page.

Any people depicted in stock imagery provided by Thinkstock are models, and such images are being used for illustrative purposes only. Certain stock imagery © Thinkstock.

This book is printed on acid-free paper.

Because of the dynamic nature of the Internet, any web addresses or links contained in this book may have changed since publication and may no longer be valid. The views expressed in this work are solely those of the author and do not necessarily reflect the views of the publisher, and the publisher hereby disclaims any responsibility for them.

Contents

Reasons for the Book and A Natural Law World View

> This book presents new knowledge and new insights into why
> and how abortion is destroying the Social Security System.
> It also explains how a world view grounded in Natural Law
> theory avoids the misunderstanding of how morality actually
> works that may be the root cause of the System's financial
> crisis.

    (An overview of the what and Why of the Book)

> This chapter explains the theory in brief, the evidence for the
> theory and why the illogical moral arguments of the abortion
> industry have contributed to the crisis.

    A Theory of the Abortion Tax

> This chapter contains the data and methodology upon which
> the theory is based. It compares the theory with a similar
> theory relating abortion to the destruction of human person
> and how abortion is destroys the Social Security System by
> destroying its revenue base – covered workers.

    Why Abortion is the Main Cause of the Abortion Tax

> The chapter explains with numbers that abortion is the main
> cause of the abortion tax because it explains more than 75
> percent of the shortage of 74 million covered workers needed

by 2037 to maintain financial solvency in the Social Security System.

(It doesn't work the way some would like it to work)
The chapter explains how morality actually works and that when the abortion industry ignores the rights of the unborn child in arguments based on "rights" it also ignores the moral consequence of abortion which could be eternal punishment. The right to choose abortion argument implies that the legal right to abortion trumps all other rights including the natural right to life which is based on illogical reasoning as the analysis in this chapter will show.

Using Information Advantage and Invented Incentive
This chapter explains how the abortion provider has a significant information advantage over most women considering an abortion and over the public in general when it comes to understanding how abortion actually works which creates the opportunity to effectively use unscrupulous tactics to attract clients and public support when the right information and tactics based on justice and truth would cost the abortion provider his fee.

Introduction

Reasons for the Book

Anyone planning on a Social Security benefit after the year 2037 very likely will be in for an economic shock. Trustees of the Social Security System have warned that the System will not be able to pay benefits at the current (2012 rate) – about $1,100 per month – because the System will not have sufficient revenue or the reserves to meet payment demands at the 100 percent level after 2037. Unless benefits are cut 25 percent (to about $825 per month) or taxes are increased (from about $300 per month per worker to $500) the System will not be able to operate at all. It is either a tax increase or a cut in benefits. One of the two or a combination of both will happen on or before 2037. This book explains the scientific evidence that the main cause of this crisis situation is the more than 50 million abortions over the past 40 years which is why the cut in benefits or increase in taxes should rightly be called an "abortion tax."

The evidence that abortion is the main cause of the Social Security System financial crisis comes from a book called Freakonomics published in 2005. The evidence that comes from Freakonomics proves how abortion actually works when it comes to the System's financial solvency problem. And understanding how abortion actually works is the key to understanding the financial crisis and why the abortion tax, although permanent, may not fix the problem.

Anyone familiar with finance knows that when an organization has to cut expenses to stay in business it has a revenue problem. And that is the problem abortions have caused for the Social Security System. Abortion destroys the System's revenue base called "covered workers." By 2037 in order to pay full benefits the System will be short an estimated 74 million covered workers. This book will show that abortions over the past 40 years most likely will have caused more than 75 percent of this shortage. The pool of covered workers paying into the System in 2037 will be missing about 53 million covered workers whose lives were aborted before they could become actual covered workers. And 98 percent of the abortions that caused this loss were for "convenience" reasons. They were not medically necessary.

Trustees of the Social Security System estimate that by 2037 about 90 million Americans will be eligible for Social Security benefits. Based on 2014 benefit data for about one third of these 90 million older and disabled Americans (about 30 million people) Social Security will account for more than 90 percent of their total income. For about two-thirds (60 million) Social Security will account for more than half their income. It doesn't take "thinking life a freak" to see the tragedy that a cut in benefits would cause for as many as 60 million or more older and disabled Americans and children dependent on Social Security for half to 90 percent of their income.

It is sad also that the abortion tax will not fix the crisis problem because it does not address the main cause. And understanding why abortion is the main cause of the crisis is inextricably related to understanding how morality actually works. Morality works according to Divine Natural Law. It does not work the way some humans, including the abortion industry, would like you to think it works. In fact the 50 million abortions in the past 40 years is reason to believe that the root cause of the crisis is a gross misunderstanding by the public especially lawmakers of how morality actually works. There also is reason to believe that the main cause of this misunderstanding is the illogical arguments of the abortion industry that have befuddled the public's thinking about how the morality of abortion actually works. The fact is the main argument of the abortion industry (the right to choose argument) is inconsistent with the Natural Rights doctrine the founding fathers wrote into the U.S. Declaration of Independence.

But given the way humans learn and think the fact is they can easily be misled by "illogical reasoning" (sometimes called tricky logic) when the issue is a little complex and the terms are not well understood. Helping people understand why the arguments of the abortion industry are illogical, morally dangerous, driven by economic incentive (money) and perhaps the root cause of why their Social Security benefits are in jeopardy is one of the more important reasons for writing this book.

A Natural Law (Judeo-Christian) World View

Both the scientific evidence and the morality issue related to abortion are based on ideas about how the real world actually works and not how some would like it to work – an idea also from Freakonomics. It is a world view grounded not only in basic economic laws but Natural Law theory also. There are "universal laws" (natural rules) – economic and moral – knowable and known by reason and/ or faith designed to govern the world and to guide people's thinking in discerning right from wrong and good behavior from bad. These laws work the same way that the physical laws of nature work. They help if you follow them and they can destroy if you don't.

Moral laws like economic laws are a part of the Natural Law. The Natural Rights doctrine is a basic tenet of the "life, liberty and pursuit of happiness" belief of traditional American culture that admonishes government not to make laws that interfere with the Natural Rights of persons. The moral laws that count are of divine origin and not of human origin which is why a government cannot give or deny an inalienable right. A human made law that is inconsistent with Natural Law is an unjust law. Morality is about good and evil; life after death; eternal reward and punishment and truth and justice. And none of these works the way people would like them to work. They work the way the Natural Law theory says they work which is the way the creator designed them to work.

The Social Security System financial crisis is not the first or only victim of illogical moral thinking. The gender imbalance in China and India is an example of what illogical thinking about morality can cause. There is an estimated 70 to 80 million more men in these countries than women because more females were aborted than males. Destroying a fetus destroys a potential future teacher, or doctor, or a future wife. So where did all the future wives go? And where will all these 70 to 80 million men find wives? Obviously it won't be in China or India. And to think that the problems in the world of human trafficking, sex slavery and forced marriages are not one of the effects of this situation (and of abortion) is illogical thinking. The Natural Law thinking the analysis in this book attempts to follow is the Natural Law theory discussed in an article and scholarly discussion called *Natural Law and Moral Catholic Theology* by Russell Hittinger in a book entitled *A Preserving Grace* edited by Michael Cromartie. Of the various "foci" of Natural Law it is the "mind of God" foci of the Natural Law that this book attempts to follow as opposed to foci of human origin. The analysis does not drill much deeper than into the basic moral precept – do good and avoid evil.

By providing a logical and scientifically valid explanation of how abortion is destroying the Social Security System and an explanation of how morality actually works based on Natural Law theory it is hoped that the economic and moral thinking can be changed to a more logical and rational approach and that the Social Security System can be saved. The crisis of 2037 is real and unavoidable but it won't save the System. Saving the System is possible but it depends upon what is done about abortion now and after 2037. The theory in this book explains why. Theories often are the cornerstones of solutions to complex problems. In most cases they at least help. The hope for the theory and discussion in this book is both. At least that is the intention.

Why Abortion Matters –
Economically and Morally

(An Overview of What the Book is about and why)

Anyone familiar with the U.S. Social Security System knows that the system is facing a financial crisis. Trustees of the System have warned that by 2037 the System will have insufficient revenue to pay benefits at the 100 percent level and no reserves to make up the deficiency in revenue. It will be necessary to cut benefits by 25 percent for about 90 million older and disabled Americans in order to be able to continue operating. Anyone familiar with abortion in America knows that there have been more than 50 million abortions in the past 40 years between 1973 and 2012. What most people probably are not familiar with is how the Social Security revenue crisis and these 50 million abortions are connected.

The connection is that abortion destroys the System's revenue base – covered workers. When abortion destroys an unborn child it also destroys what that unborn child would have become some 20 years later. The fact is the number of contributors to the System is about 50 million covered workers fewer than what it would have been had there not been 50 million abortions in the past 40 years. The U.S. Social Security System is a "pay-as-you-go" system. Benefit payments each year are limited to revenue each year. The way the System is structured it takes the "tax revenue" from about <u>three</u> covered workers to pay the "benefit costs" of <u>one</u> beneficiary. This "dependency ratio" as it is called must be about 3 to 1 to maintain financial solvency and pay benefits at the current 100 percent level. By 2037 abortion by destroying covered workers is the main cause of why the dependency ratio will drop to 2 to 1. With only two workers to pay the benefits of one beneficiary either the tax rate must increase or the benefit must be cut in order for the System to stay in business. If benefits are cut or taxes increased millions of Americans will be forced into poverty.

And there is scientific evidence to prove that abortion most likely is the main cause of why the number of covered workers is not growing fast enough to meet the growing expense demands of the System and why millions of Americans will be faced with an "abortion tax" by 2037. The evidence apparently has not been recognized before because there is a significant "latency period" between abortion and its effects on various population cohorts. Because of this latency effect abortion in the 1970s would not begin to affect the Social Security System until the 1990s or 2000s. Also a problem in recognizing the connection between abortion and the crisis is the fact that the effect of abortion is reflected in the growth rate of the System's revenue base – covered workers – rather than absolute growth which is a measure not readily transparent. The actual number of covered workers has increased each year. However the growth rate in covered workers has diminished – been less each year – since the 1990s. The latency or "time lag" feature is a significant feature of how abortion actually works and is considered one of the breakthrough discoveries in Freakonomics that led to the discovery of how abortion affects the Social Security System.

The dependency ratio in 1975 was 3.3. By 2010 it had dropped to 3.0. Abortions in 1980 were twice what they were in 1970. The number of abortions averaged about 1.5 million per year from 1975 to 1990. Given the "latency period" associated with abortion it was the abortions in the 1975 to 1990 period that caused the dependency ratio to begin declining in 2010 and why it will be down to 2 to 1 by 2037.

The significance of what a falling dependency ratio reflects is explained in a bulletin by the Social Security System issued in 2010 entitled <u>Future Financial Status of the Social Security Program</u> in the section – "Future Changes for the Social Security Program."

> For the past 35 years, there have been about 3.3 workers per beneficiary (consistent with the ratio of 30 beneficiaries per 100 workers). After 2030, the ratio will be two workers per beneficiary (consistent with 50 beneficiaries per 100 workers). With the average worker benefit currently at about $1,000 per month, 3.3 workers would need to contribute about $300 each per month to provide a $1,000 benefit. But after the population age distribution has shifted to have just two workers per beneficiary, each worker would need to contribute $500 to provide the same $1,000 benefit. http://www.ssa.gov/policy/docs/ssb/ v70n3/v70n3p111.html

The statement says the dependency ratio "will" be 2 to 1 after 2030 not that it may be. Also the population age shift is essentially the fact that there are fewer younger people in the current generation – and fewer covered workers - than the last generation but more beneficiaries (covered workers from several generations ago) and consequently a lower dependency ratio. This "time lag" situation is believed to be the main reason for why the connection has not been recognized before. By 2030 the lower growth rate in covered workers compared to a somewhat larger growth rate in beneficiaries (caused by abortions 20 to 30 years ago) is what will cause the dependency ratio to fall to 2 to 1. Of the several factors that can cause the particular population distribution shift in this instance the main cause most likely is abortion as the theory in this book will explain.

The falling dependency ratio reflects how abortion affects the System's revenue. Abortion causes the "growth rate" in the System's revenue base – covered workers – to be less than the growth rate in the System's expense base – older and disabled American beneficiaries. The revenue base simply is not "growing" fast enough to meet increasing payment demands. To be sure there are factors other than or in addition to abortion that could cause the dependency ratio to fall but none explains as much of the fall as abortion does. Two of the other causes mentioned by Trustees of the System are the falling fertility rate and the baby boomer retirement surge. Although the fertility rate during the baby boom years (about 3.7 from 1946 to 1964) dropped significantly to about 2.1 from what it was during their parent's generation the fertility rate for the generations after the baby boomers (about 2.1 before 1973) it has remained about the same since. In fact Trustees project it to change very little for the next 50 years. The fertility rate explains some but not a significant amount of the covered worker growth situation. It is a factor but not the main factor. And as it is projected to remain about the same for the next five decades it is not the main problem.

The surge in baby boom retirees likewise is not considered a significant cause of the drop in the dependency ratio. The System began experiencing operating deficits and using reserves to make up the deficiency in revenue in 2010. The surge did not begin until 2011 and it will have run its course by 2038. The problem reflected in the declining dependency ratio was there before the baby boom surge and it will be there for decades after. In fact the dependency ratio by 2085 is projected to be only 1.9 to 1 with the 25 percent cut in benefits in 2037. It was projected to be 2.1 to 1 at the end of the baby boom surge (2038). The baby boom retirement surge explains some but not a significant amount of the covered worker growth situation. As will be shown later in this book abortion explains most of the covered worker growth problem.

Trustees of the System explain the falling dependency ratio in terms of a "demographic shift" which in economics is a transition to lower fertility rates and lower death rates which would result in fewer contributing workers and more retirees. Although abortion is not mentioned as a factor in the "demographic shift," the fact is an increase in the abortion rate has the same effect as a decline in the fertility rate. And the abortion rate more than doubled in the 1980s compared to what it was in the 1970s and remained about one and a half times greater through the 1990s. Abortion in the 1970s, 1980s and 1990s more than likely explains most of the declining dependency ratio since 2010. The reality is that 50 million abortions will destroy almost the same number of potential covered workers. It is true also that although the impact of this aspect of the "demographic shift" on the growth of covered workers should be obvious the fact is it may not have been as the analysis in later chapters will show.

There also are factors other than abortion, fertility rates and the baby boom surge that could impact the solvency situation as well as the System's revenue including the average income of workers, hours worked, labor force participation rate and the tax rate but none of these as reflected in the Trustees reports is considered a significant cause of the falling dependency ratio as well. It appears that the impact of these factors have been considered by Trustees in their projections and included in the prediction that the benefit cut will need to be 25 percent. Also given the fact that Trustees have warned that a benefit cut will be necessary by 2037 to maintain financial solvency it appears that whatever change there will be in these factors none individually or as a group is likely to cause a material change in the System's revenue situation. Considering all the factors that could impact the situation abortion most likely is the main cause of the Social Security financial crisis although other factors may explain some of the crisis.

The effects of abortion on the growth rate of covered workers and beneficiaries and how abortion affects the "covered worker gap" and the solvency crisis is demonstrated by the data in Charts I and II. The data for actual workers available (shown as actual in Chart I) and beneficiaries is taken from projections by Trustees of the System. The number of workers required in order for the System to have the revenue to pay full benefits (shown as required in Chart I) is determined by multiplying the Trustee's beneficiary projections by what is considered the "required dependency ratio" and the dependency ratio in 2010 – 2.9 to 1. From 1990 to 2009 the actual number of workers paying revenue into the System was greater than the number required for full benefits and was growing at about the same rate. However the growth rate began to diminish in the 1990s. In 2010 the required number and actual number were equal. There was no gap. After 2010 the actual number of workers paying revenue into the System is less than the number required for full benefits and growing at a slower rate.

Chart I
Trend in Covered Worker Gap by select years 1990 to 2037
(millions)

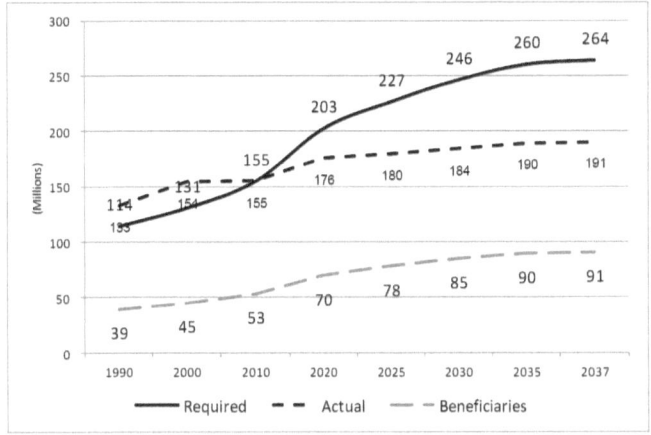

The "covered worker gap" is caused by differences in the "latency effect" of abortion on the covered worker population compared to the beneficiary population. The latency affect of abortion on covered workers is the time between the abortion and when the person would have entered the labor force - about 20 years. It is about 65 years on beneficiaries – the time between abortion and the time the person retires. In a pay-as-you-go system (as the U.S. System is) the growth rate in revenue diminishes four or five decades sooner than the growth rate in expenses. These differences in the latency periods are reflected in the decline in the dependency ratio from about 2.9 to 1 in 2010 to 2 to 1 by 2037. The surge of abortions in the 80s, 90s and 2000s averaging 1.6, 1.4 and 1.6 million annually respectively caused the growth rate of covered workers to begin to diminish beginning in the 1990s. They will not cause the growth rate in the beneficiary population to begin to diminish until after 2038 (65 years after 1973) as those born in the 1970s and later begin to retire but will be missing those potential retirees who were aborted in the 1970s and later. Thus the abortions that have already happened through 2010 and those that are projected to happen by 2017 are considered the main cause of the widening "covered worker gap" up to 2037 and logically a significant gap after 2037. Trustees project that by 2085 the dependency ratio still will not exceed 2 to 1. The implications of this fact are discussed in Chapter 2. One significant implication is that the abortion tax (cut in benefits or increase in taxes) is a permanent feature of the Social Security System.

The significance of abortion on the crisis situation the theory in this book explains is illustrated in Chart II. Projections by Trustees of the System indicate that by 2037 the beneficiary pool will total about 91 million and the actual covered worker pool about 191 million – a dependency ratio of 2 to 1. However in order to pay full benefits 91 million beneficiaries will require a "pool" of about 264 million workers (assuming a dependency ratio of 2.9 to 1). The System will be short about 73 million workers to be able to pay full benefits. The evidence presented in this book is that by 2037 abortion will have destroyed 56 million of the 73 million covered workers required for the System to be able to pay full benefits (see Chart II).

Chart II
The Covered Worker Gap caused by Abortion by 2037
(millions)

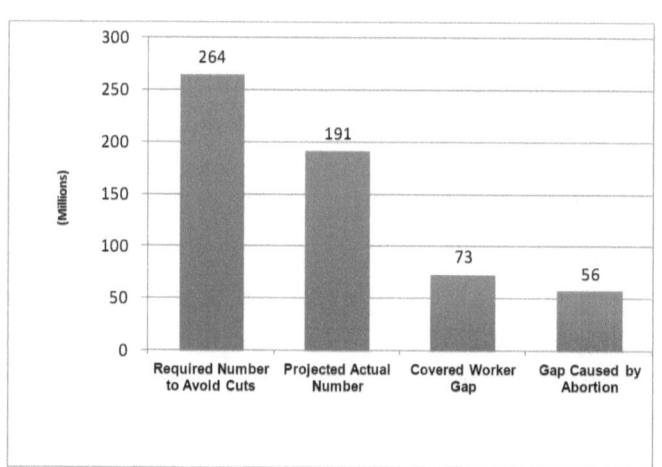

In order for the System to avoid financial insolvency benefits will need to be cut 25 percent or taxes increased. As is explained in Chapter 2 none of the factors other than abortion individually or collectively explain as much as the decline in the dependency ratio from 3 to 1 to 2 to 1 by 2037 as abortion explains. Abortion is not the only cause of the crisis but it is the main cause.

The scientific evidence for the validity of this argument and that abortion most likely is the main cause of this "covered worker gap" is a theory in Freakonomics explaining how abortion in the 1970s was linked to a drop in crime rates in the 1990s. The significance of the theory with respect to the Social Security financial situation is that the linkage between abortion and crime rates in the abortion/crime rate theory is essentially the same as how abortion is linked to the Social Security financial crisis. Based on a method called "reasoning by analogy" the theory in Freakonomics is considered evidence of the validity of the theory in this book.

The "reasoning by analogy methodology" is explained in more detail in Chapter Two. The method is explained in the Stanford Encyclopedia of Philosophy at http://plato.stanford.edu/entries/reasoning-analogy/ as a type of inductive reasoning and "…has played an important, but sometimes mysterious, role in a wide range of problem-solving contexts." As the analysis in Chapter Two will show there are "strong" similarities in the known elements of the two theories supporting the conclusion that there are strong similarities in the unknown elements as well. The inference in the abortion/crime rate theory is that abortion is the main cause of the "shrinkage" in the criminal population and thus the drop in crime rates. The similar inference in the abortion/ covered worker theory is that abortion most likely is the main cause of the "shrinkage" in the covered worker population and thus a drop in the growth rate of revenue and the resulting financial crisis.

Analogical reasoning, arguably, was used by Freakonomics' authors to explain how and why abortion reduced crime. The scientific method was used to prove that the linkage between abortion and crime rates was real and not due to chance. However the explanation of how and why abortion reduced crime was based, arguably, on analogical reasoning. Authors introduced a term called "unwantedness" which in the context of abortion means "not wanting" a child or a person. And a person not wanted has a good chance of becoming a criminal according to the unwantedness thinking. The unwantedness explanation, arguably, is based on analogical reasoning because it is based on the similarity between conditions in the U.S. in the 1970s through the 1990s and conditions in Romania and other Eastern European countries with similar experiences with abortion (see the discussion in Freakonomics, p 136 to 139).

> As far as crime is concerned, it turns out that not all children are born equal. Not even close. Decades of studies have shown that a child born into an adverse family environment is far more likely than other children to become a criminal (Freakonomics, p 6).

In this context according to Freakonomics the "environmental conditions" that led women to have abortions also caused young men to become criminals. The logical extension of what authors of Freakonomics seemed to be arguing is that crime rates would drop because abortion eliminated actual criminals. Since teenagers and adults commit crimes and abortion does not eliminate either then it is necessary that abortion eliminate potential criminals before they become actual criminals. Thus, arguably, by analogical reasoning, authors of Freakonomics concluded that less unwantedness would lead to fewer potential criminals, which would lead to fewer actual criminals which logically would lead to less crime.

Expressed in "syllogistic argument" form using the term "unwantedness" as it was used in Freakonomics the abortion/crime rate theory (as it is stated in Freakonomics) is: legalized abortion led to "less unwantedness; unwantedness leads to high crime; legalized abortion therefore led to less crime." (p 139). The statement, arguably, implies that abortion destroys unwantedness by destroying the thing unwanted (the unborn person).

With some modification in propositions from positive to negative form (e.g. if unwantedness leads to high crime then less unwantedness leads to less crime) and modification in the sequence of terms, none of which change the conclusion and the argument itself, the abortion/crime rate theory in syllogistic form is:

> Less unwantedness leads to less crime.
> Legalized abortion leads to less unwantedness.
> Legalized abortion leads to less crime.

An alternative expression of the theory by authors of Freakonomics, arguably, substitutes the term "potential criminal" for "crime." Since only criminals commit crimes fewer criminals would mean less crime. Also, arguably, in order for there to be fewer criminals there would need to be fewer "potential criminals" which essentially is what the theory in Freakonomics proves. The alternative term changes only the "terms" of the syllogism but does not change the inference that abortion destroys human persons with potential.

> All unwanted children were potential criminals
> All aborted children were unwanted children.
> All aborted children were potential criminals.

All three parts of this syllogism – major and minor premises and conclusion – are true based upon the research and theory in

Freakonomics. It also is true based on Natural Law reasoning. Logically all children – born or unborn – have the potential of becoming criminals. Also, logically all aborted children were unwanted. The premises are true because of their consistency with the theory in Freakonomics and their consistency with Natural Law theory.

The similarity between the abortion/crime rate theory and the abortion/covered worker theory is demonstrated when the abortion/ covered worker theory also is expressed in syllogistic form. A fetus is a human person with potentiality. A fetus can be a potential covered worker or a potential criminal or both. The abortion/covered worker theory expressed in the same syllogistic form shows that abortion destroys the System's revenue base (covered workers) and thus adversely affects the System's revenue. It shows how abortion and the Social Security financial crisis are linked:

> All unwanted (fetuses) unborn children are potential covered workers.
> All aborted (fetuses) unborn children were unwanted (fetuses) children.
> All aborted (fetuses) unborn children were potential covered workers.

Actually the same logic applies to born children as well as unborn children. The scientific evidence for the validity of the premises in the abortion/covered worker theory is the finding in the abortion/crime rate theory in Freakonomics. Both the major and minor premises by analogical reasoning are proven true scientifically by the theory in Freakonomics.

The connection between "potential human persons" and "actual human persons" also is explained by the abortion/crime rate theory in Freakonomics. The relevant cohort of "actual criminals" discussed in Freakonomics was less because the pool of "potential criminals" was less.

> In the early 1990s, just when the first cohort of children born after Roe v. Wade was hitting its late teen years – the years when young men enter their criminal prime – the rate of crime began to fall. What this cohort was missing, of course, were the children who stood the greatest chance of becoming criminals. (p139).

Logically the cohort of "actual covered workers" was less for the same and/or similar reason. It was missing the covered workers that were aborted some 20 years or so earlier. The theory upon which these propositions are fundamental is developed and explained in Chapter Two.

One of what might be called a "hidden side" of abortion is a phenomenon referred to in Freakonomics as the "replication effect" of abortion (Freakonomics p 141). This effect has a significant impact on the covered worker "gap" referred to above. The replication affect is the idea that children tend to duplicate or "replicate" the characteristics of their parents. A woman who is a cowgirl tends to have a daughter who also becomes a cowgirl. Among the 24 million abortions during the 70s and 80s there were theoretically 12 million potential mothers who were aborted that would have had children including daughters who most likely would have copied (replicated) the attributes and behavior of their parent. They would have had daughters who would have had children some of whom would grow up to become criminals. But some of them would have grown up to become covered workers or cowgirls.

The concept of "unwantedness" also used in the abortion/ crime rate theory in Freakonomics has implications for the Social Security covered worker "gap." From an abortion perspective there logically is similarity between "unwantedness" and "inconvenience." Arguably an unborn child is "unwanted" if it is "inconvenient" at the moment. Both unwantedness and inconvenience can result in the same outcome for the unborn child. The implication, however, is that a pregnancy can be inconvenient to a woman who is not necessarily poor, relatively uneducated, single, etc. but one living in an environment relatively friendly for normal growth and development of the child. If the aborted child is female in this situation then the replication effect predicts a loss of covered workers rather than criminals. Regardless of whether it is unwantedness or inconvenience each female abortion destroys a potential covered worker, a potential mother and all the potential covered workers the mother and her daughter and granddaughter, etc. would have produced all of whom would have the potential of becoming productive members of the covered worker population.

But the argument in this book is that abortion is the "main cause" of the crisis. Logically in order for abortion to be the main cause of the "covered worker gap" and the main cause of the crisis it is necessary that abortion explain most of the gap between the "actual" number of covered workers and the number "required" to pay benefits at the 100 percent level. The data for the "actual" number of covered workers and beneficiaries are from projections by Trustees of the System. The "required" number of covered workers is the product of the projected number of beneficiaries times what is called a "required or natural dependency ratio" which is 2.9 to 1 as indicated by data from Trustees reports. In fact all the data for the projection are in Trustee's reports.

The covered worker gap analysis is discussed in Chapter Three and will show that by 2037 the "gap" will total about 73 million covered workers. The system will require about 73 million more workers than the actual number available in order to pay benefits at the 100 percent level. Also the abortion/covered worker theory will show that about 75 percent of the "gap" (about 56 million covered workers) most likely is explained by abortion. Most likely 75 percent is a greater percentage of the effect of abortion on the covered worker pool than it was on the criminal pool in the abortion/ crime rate theory. Other factors such as fertility rates, the labor force participation rate and time lags are considered in the calculations in Chapter three.

In addition to the scientific evidence from Freakonomics the validity of the theory also is supported by statements by Trustees of the System such as the "demographic shift" statement and statements reflecting rather drastic solutions to the reality that a true crisis exists and what it will take to deal with the crisis. In a report titled The Future Financial Status of the Social Security Program in the introduction section there is the following statement that confirms the solvency situation and the proposed solution.

> The Social Security Board of Trustees project that changes equivalent to an immediate reduction in benefits of about 13 percent, or an immediate increase in the combined payroll tax rate from 12.4 percent to 14.4 percent, or some combination of these changes, would be sufficient to allow full payment of the scheduled benefits for the next 75 years. http://www. ssa.gov/policy/docs/ssb/v70n3/v70n3p111.html

The statement also confirms why the solution proposed by Trustees is called an abortion tax as either remedy will reduce income for some which is essentially what a tax does.

Regardless of how one feels about abortion morally the fact is people may not realize that abortion is destroying the U.S. Social Security System. However illogical thinking about morality in general and the morality of abortion in particular can be the root cause of a financial crisis and perhaps is the root cause of the current financial crisis Social Security faces. Aborting the lives of a million unborn persons per year by one generation obviously will cause one million fewer teachers, doctors and workers of all kinds for later generations. But one million abortions per year probably would not happen unless people either do not understand how morality actually works or they understand but ignore how it actually works. Morality works the way the Divine Natural Moral Law says it works. How it works is not determined by human design. The truth is the arguments of those who support abortion are not based on basic precepts of morality as found in the Natural Moral Law and they are not supported by empirical evidence. In fact the arguments amount to illogical thinking because in most cases the premises of the arguments are not true and the argument itself is not true. To be sure there are circumstances contributing to the confusion. However it also is true that people can easily be confused by the illogical arguments of the abortion industry.

When the premises of the main pro-abortion argument – right to choose argument -- are analyzed for consistency with the Natural Law it is evident that the premises are not based on true and logical reasoning. The argument is not based on basic Laws of Morality; they are not based on empirical evidence and the conclusions are not based on the rules of sound argument. They are not consistent with how the real world of morality actually works. Rather it is a morality based on how the industry would like morality to work. But one way the world does work is that people not as familiar with the Laws of Morality as perhaps they should be can be befuddled by arguments designed to befuddle.– a situation that abortion proponents could and have taken advantage of.

As used in Science a "law" is a "rule" that is a guide to how things work. A moral law is a rule to guide behavior toward an ultimate and good purpose. Laws of economics serve the same purpose. However there are laws of human origin and laws of divine origin. The latter are called Natural Laws. There can be unjust laws of human origin but not unjust laws of divine origin. A Natural Law has universal application. A civil law may not. Morality based on Natural Law behaves the same for all persons at all places at all times. Violate laws of nature and the result can be disaster. Try to fly off a 10 story building in the U.S., China or anywhere and the result will be the same – probably death. And most people would know not to attempt to fly off a 10 story building because they know "naturally" that it would violate the Laws (rules) of Nature. Natural Moral Laws work the same way. They are "rules" of how persons are to treat each other that have universal application. The unjust killing of another human person is a violation of the Natural Moral Law for all persons, at all places and at all times. Violations can be disastrous. The difference is the penalty for violating Laws of Nature (e.g. gravity) can be experienced and observed and happen before death. On the other hand the penalty for violating Natural Moral Laws (e.g. unjust killing) generally is not observable and happens in life after death. The way both types of laws work is discoverable by reason and reason guides how they are to be used and obeyed. To argue that an opportunity to do injustice to another is morally good is impossible.

In many cases when an argument based on sound moral reasoning cannot be made the argument is based on emotion which usually involves some type of tricky logic. Authors of Freakonomics point out that parents often use this approach with their children (e.g. to get their children to eat vegetables.) Supporters of abortion argue that abortion is a matter of a woman's right or a woman's health. Generally these arguments are not based on sound moral reasoning and are not backed by reliable scientific evidence. However people tend to be emotional about rights and health issues. Thus these argument can be effective because the morality issue of abortion is not easy to understand and can easily be misunderstood especially when the argument is "emotionally charged." The mechanics of an abortion and the rules of morality are not topics that most people deal with on a regular basis. And for the most part they are technical and logical and not emotional. Add the fact that the abortion industry has an incentive for making the issue confusing and the result is illogical thinking about an issue that can lead to disaster – economic and moral.

Whether a person's misunderstanding of the issue and being misled by the abortion industry's argument to keep abortion alive is due to his/her own lack of diligence or the deliberate "obfuscation" of the moral issue by those who profit from abortion the result is the same – illogical thinking. The problem with solutions based on illogical thinking is that they usually are wrong.

History is full of examples of illogical moral thinking. It could be argued that the main cause of the Civil War, apartheid and the Nazi treatment of the Jews was illogical moral thinking about slavery and the dignity of human persons all of which were violations of the Natural Moral Law. Logically there are consequences to violating the Natural Moral Law just as there are consequences to violating the Natural Physical Laws. The financial crisis in the Social Security System is a result of violating Natural Moral Law. The Social Security financial crisis could be what economists call the "opportunity cost" of 50 million abortions. But that many abortions do not happen unless there is significant misunderstanding about the morality of abortion.

Arguments framed in "rights" and "health" can be confusing if one is not familiar with these concepts and to some extent the scientific method that demands proof for the truth of an argument. Illogical thinking is not uncommon when it comes to a complex issue as abortion is.

In a later chapter the arguments of the abortion industry in support of abortion will be examined for their consistency or lack of consistency with basic objective moral standards found in the Devine Natural Law which focuses on how God thinks and not on how humans think. *(see A Preserving Grace* edited by Michael Cromartie.) Thus the approach to analyzing the arguments of the abortion industry is substantially logical and only somewhat biblical. How morality works is not a matter of individual preference or personal belief. In fact the precepts are not of human origin at all. And to discover and understand them it is necessary to use sound logical thinking guided by moral precepts considered natural to human persons.

To demonstrate this consistency or inconsistency with objective morality the analysis will focus on what is considered the key arguments of the abortion industry – right to choose and women's health. The arguments are expressed in syllogistic form in order to make transparent the terms of the argument including the premises upon which the argument is based. It is the premises of an argument that must be consistent with objective morality (and true) in order for the conclusion or inference for an argument to be true. If the premises are inconsistent with objective moral precepts (and false) then the conclusion is false. To be morally sound the basic moral precepts expressed and/or implied in the argument must be consistent with scientific evidence and the moral precepts from Natural Moral Law. Since the Natural Law and Scripture have the same divine author the moral precepts in the Natural Law and Scripture are the same. The use of syllogisms discloses whether the argument is logical or illogical and in fact why it is either.

The analysis of the morality argument of the abortion industry extends only to two basic moral precepts considered the two most basic standards and the two for which an understanding is necessary to gain a basic understanding of why the abortion industry's morality argument is considered morally illogical. The two precepts are justice and truth. They are violated by "unjust killing" and "false witness" or lying and they both have Scripture and Natural Law foundations. In the "rich young man" narrative in Scripture Jesus' first words in response to the rich young man's question of what he must do to gain eternal life (and logically avoid eternal punishment) was: do not kill! Both killing and bearing false witness are violations of "objective" standards of morality and both are prohibited in the 10 Commandments.

To assure objectivity in the analysis the analysis will focus on the "right to choose" argument as it was defined and discussed in Freakonomics. It is believed the argument capitalizes on the fact that many people most likely are not fully aware of the difference between legal rights and Natural rights or laws of human origin and those of divine or natural origin. Arguably the way authors of Freakonomics interpreted the argument is that the "right to choose" abortion "trumps any other factor" (p144). There are several moral implications and sources of confusion in an argument of this type as, arguably, the analysis in Freakonomics demonstrates. One is that the unborn human person has no rights because it is worthless and something or someone worthless, it is implied, has no rights. Also "any other factor" logically implies all other rights. Thus the argument implies or assumes that abortion is a natural right and that a right of human origin trumps a right of divine origin. The problem is that this line of thinking is inconsistent with Natural Law: a right of human origin does not trump a right of divine origin. For the "right to choose" argument to be a "logically sound moral argument" the premises of the argument and the conclusion would need to be consistent with objective moral standards found in the Natural Law. The analysis in Chapter four will show that they are not.

There is another aspect of the morality issue that becomes apparent when one digs into the situation to understand how and why befuddling arguments are made in the first place. In dealing with an abortion provider the young woman also is vulnerable to what is referred to in Freakonomics as unscrupulous tactics used by unscrupulous operators to attract clients. Such unscrupulous tactics are considered violations of the "false witness" moral precept and a violation based on the Natural Law as well as the 10 Commandments in Scripture.

Two of these tactics are what are referred to in Freakonomics as "information advantage" and "invented incentive" discussed in Freakonomics on pages 67 and 21 respectively. With respect to information advantage abortion providers have the "relevant information" that the young woman does not have. There were theories in Freakonomics, arguably, based both on the scientific method and analogical reasoning that explained that sellers would use unscrupulous tactics to attract clients when telling the truth might mean losing a fee. These theories, arguably, apply to the situation of the abortion provider dealing with a young woman considering an abortion. If the abortion provider is fully truthful about his service the young woman may change her mind and cost the provider his fee. Providing tainted information is considered lying morally although it may be considered good but unethical business. The way the real world actually works the moral incentive often gets overridden by the economic incentive an idea also found in Freakonomics.

The invented incentive tactic is based on the fact that abortion is an emotionally charged issue and fear is usually the emotion the young woman is dealing with. As it turns out one of the most powerful emotions is fear. And invented or created incentives usually are based on fear. Since most young women facing their first unexpected pregnancy are "emotionally distraught" they are vulnerable to "irrational expectations" either those created themselves or those created for them by, in this instance, the abortion provider. Likewise the public is vulnerable to the misuse of invented incentive as there is a natural inclination to fear or be against a "tragic situation" which is how the abortion provider most likely presents the situation. An irrational expectation is something that is not likely or logically going to happen. But the fear of it, if it did happen, can be a powerful motivator!

Why would unscrupulous arguments like the right to choose trumps all other rights and unscrupulous tactics like "information advantage" and "invented incentive" be used? The reason as explained in Freakonomics is "economic incentive." There are people who make money off abortion. The abortion provider has an "economic incentive" to make abortion happen. The fact is, according to Freakonomics, economic incentive can override moral incentive. In this instance it could make the abortion provider and resolute supporters of abortion even ignore or minimize the moral consequences of immoral behavior – the risk of hell – in the pursuit of profit. The economic incentive for the abortion industry is substantial. The industry's take from abortions is about $1.0 billion annually including about $500 million it gets in government grants. It seems clear that abortion providers have an economic incentive to keep abortion alive. The reality is that keeping it alive means keeping the public and the young woman considering an abortion befuddled about the moral issues involved.

When authors of Freakonomics discussed the morality issue they suggested, arguably, that morality might be a matter of "how some would like it (the world) to work" rather than "how the real world actually works." Befuddling the public about the morality of abortion is not a difficult thing to do. Arguments involving legal and natural rights such as "the right to choose," and arguments involving medical science such as the "women's health" argument can easily be made confusing. How and why this is a reality is explored in Chapter Four.

This book is about a theory, and the scientific evidence for the theory, linking abortion to the Social Security financial crisis and why abortion is considered the main cause of the crisis. The book is written from a world view perspective of how the world actually works including especially how laws of morality actually work. It is written also from a Natural Law (Christian) view of how the real world actually works. It develops the idea that the root cause of the crisis is a misunderstanding of how the morality of abortion actually works to which the illogical arguments of the abortion industry has contributed significantly. It also develops the argument that abortion providers might use unscrupulous tactics, known to be used by some unscrupulous professionals, to induce young women to have abortions based on the idea that a young woman faced with her first unplanned pregnancy is highly vulnerable to such tactics.

Where have all the Covered Workers Gone?

A Theory of the Abortion Tax

This rhetorical question (where have all the covered workers gone) comes from a similar question in Freakonomics (the Title to Chapter 4 p 117). When authors of Freakonomics asked the question "where have all the criminals gone" they recognized, arguably, that the essence of abortion is that it destroys the benefit or cost of what that person would have contributed when he/she reached adulthood. Obviously abortion does not destroy criminals. It destroys unborn children who have the potential of growing up to become criminals.

This fact is important because the way abortion affects the Social Security System is somewhat unique and somewhat hidden. It is both unique and hidden because of a "time lag" factor between abortion and its effects. The fact is there is a time lag of about 20 years between the time of the abortion and the time the aborted child would have become a member of the covered worker population. It takes another 40 to 50 years before the aborted child would have become a member of the beneficiary population of the System. Abortion causes both the System's revenue and its expenses to be less or grow at a lesser rate but it affects revenue four to five decades before it affects expenses. This situation combined with a low birth rate, a falling fertility rate and an increasing abortion rate means the effect of abortion on revenue can cause a serious imbalance between revenue and expense in a pay-as-you-go system as the U.S. System is. The reason for this imbalance can easily be overlooked or "hidden" unless one is fully aware of how abortion actually works. Given little or no change in other factors the System's growth rate in revenue could be less than its growth rate in expenses for a period of time causing the System to experience financial solvency problems.

This situation means the effect of legalizing abortion can be hidden as well. In fact according to Freakonomics "legalizing abortion changed everything" (p 117). Perhaps the most unintended change was the destruction of the Social Security System. The trend in the financial situation of the Social Security System since the 1990s has been a slower growth rate in covered workers. The result is a trend toward financial insolvency. It is a situation clearly recognized by Trustees of the System in their 2012 report and in other reports including a report entitled the *Future Financial Status of the Social Security System* published in 2010. In fact Trustees clearly recognize that fewer live births each year is most likely the problem.

> What is notable is that the strong upward shift in both this ratio and in the cost rate is permanent; it does not come back down to a lower level after the large baby boom generation dies off. The permanence of this shift was not caused by the existence of the baby boom generation; instead, the permanent shift was caused by the substantial and apparently permanent drop in birth rates that followed the baby boom births.(p 16/21). http://www.ssa.gov/policy/docs/ssb/v70n3/v70n3p111.html

It is believed that the statement is about 90 percent correct. It would be 100 percent correct if it gave recognition to the trend in abortions over the past 40 years as a key factor in why the birth rate has dropped to a lower and permanent level. The drop in the fertility rate is mentioned but the reality is an increase in the abortion rate has the same effect as a drop in the fertility rate. And the fact is abortion rates more than doubled in the 1980s while fertility rates changed very little.

The trend toward insolvency will continue until the System is destroyed unless the cause of the problem reflected by the trend is eliminated. What happens in 2037 is a milestone in the trend. The benefit cut or tax increase that will happen in 2037 will make it possible for the System to continue but without the tax increase only with a significant slash in benefits. However, unless the cause of the destruction of covered workers over the past 40 years is not the focus of solutions to the crisis the trend will continue until tragically the System is gone. Benefit cuts and increases in payroll tax rates have their limits. It is hoped that the question "where have all the covered workers gone" is not a question rhetorically explaining what "happened" to the Social Security System. But realistically benefit cuts and tax increases have their limits? And realistically – so should abortion.

It is not clear that legalizing abortion was designed to accomplish anything economically sound. Although it was clear to some, it probably was not clear to many including policy makers that legalizing abortion would have the destructive effects that it would have on the U.S. Social Security System. The fact is destroying covered workers means less revenue to the Social Security System and a declining growth rate in revenue combined with an increasing growth rate in expenses is a prescription for financial insolvency.

The theory developed in this chapter explains this situation. The evidence for the validity of the "abortion/covered worker theory" (as it is called in this book) is a theory in Freakonomics explaining a similar relationship between abortion and criminals. The fact is abortion destroys human persons. The theory in Freakonomics explained the relationship between abortion and the destruction of certain types of human persons – criminals – but the theory applies to other types of human persons including covered workers, teachers, etc. When abortion destroys a fetus it destroys whatever that fetus would have been to society when it reached adulthood.

According to the theory in Freakonomics abortions in the 1970s were the main cause of a drop in crime rates in the 1990s. Crime rates went down because abortion destroyed potential criminals before they became actual criminals. The situation with respect to the Social Security financial crisis is highly similar if not the same: abortion destroys potential covered workers before they become actual coverered workers. In effect abortion destroys actual covered workers. Actual covered workers are the revenue base of the System. Based on its similarity to the theory in Freakonomics the theory in this book is that abortions in the 70s and 80s most likely are the main cause of the declining growth rate in the System's "covered worker pool" in the 1990s and beyond.

The economic approach in Freakonomics was as authors point out an approach based on how the "real world actually works" (p 13). Thus it is an approach based on numbers, logic and reasoning and not on religious beliefs or scripture. It is science! Thus the theory in this book is essentially the same based on analogical reasoning. It is science not religion.

Analogical reasoning also is a scientific method of analysis. It is considered similar to the "right numbers measured the right way" approach in Freakonomics. It is a matter of using the "right theory applied the right way." The right theory is analogous to the right numbers.

> *Analogical reasoning* is any type of thinking that relies upon an analogy. An *analogical argument* is an explicit representation of a form of analogical reasoning that cites accepted similarities between two systems to support the conclusion that some further similarity exists. In general (but not always), such arguments belong in the category of inductive reasoning, since their conclusions do not follow with certainty but are only supported with varying degrees of strength. The explicit use of analogical arguments, since antiquity, has been a distinctive feature of scientific, philosophical and legal reasoning. http://plato.stanford.edu/entries/reasoning-analogy/#Exa

Notwithstanding the complexity of analogical reasoning its use is common in scientific analysis. From a scientific perspective the basic task using analogical reasoning is to demonstrate that the similarities between the proposed theory and the theory with which it is considered similar are indeed strong. To say that something is the "most likely" cause of an effect is similar to but not the same as saying that it is highly probably that the relationship is not due to chance but is real or actual. Basically any scientific argument is based on reason. The evidence is proof of the theory's consistency with how the real world actually works. The evidence for the validity of the abortion/crime rate theory was the measured relationship between abortion and crime rates. The unknown factor in the abortion/covered worker theory is "how much" of the diminishing growth in the covered worker pool is caused by abortion. But since abortion was the main cause of the drop in crime rates it is logical to infer, based on analogical reasoning, that it is "most likely" the main cause of the diminishing growth rate in covered workers during the same time period. The inference is that the two inferences are similar based on the similarity between the known features of the two theories.

The first task in developing the theory in this book is to analyze and explain the data upon which the validity of the theory is based. The analysis will demonstrate that the similarities between abortion and crime rates and between abortion and the growth rate of the Social Security System's revenue base – covered workers - are considered clear, strong, relevant and comprehensive which is what proving validity using analogical reasoning requires. The strength of these observed similarities is evidence that the degree of correlation between abortion and its effect on the covered worker pool, if it were known, would be about the same as abortion's affect on crime rates.

One of the stronger and more comprehensive similarities is in the actual cause and effect relationship itself. Both the cause and the effect in both theories is essentially the same. The cause is abortion. The effect is the destruction of human persons with potentiality as will be explained in this chapter. By causing the destruction of potential criminals abortion reduced the pool of actual criminals 20 years later. If there are fewer criminals there would be less crime given that the number of crimes per criminal remained about the same. Similarly if there are fewer potential covered workers there will be fewer actual covered workers 20 years later and the growth rate in revenue would diminish as it has.

There also is strong similarity in the situation with the "time lag" factor. As discussed in Freakonomics there is a significant "time lag" between abortion and its effects including its affects on social outcomes like crime rates and the Social Security crisis situation. The "time lag" factor is the fact that some of the effects of abortion do not show up for many years, even decades after the abortion. The significance of this factor is that it most likely is the reason the relationship between abortion and its effects on the Social Security financial crisis has remained essentially "hidden" as it did in the abortion/crime rate relationship. It also is a reason why the relationship might be difficult to understand. As pointed out in Freakonomics people tend to believe "proximate" causes (even when they are wrong) over "latent" and/or "remote" causes. The time lag factor between abortion and crime rates in the abortion/crime rate theory was about 20 years. It is about the same between abortion and the time a child becomes a member of the labor force – also about 20 years.

The time lag factor also has the effect of producing what Freakonomics referred to as "conventional wisdom" that "frequently is wrong." According to Freakonomics there were seven major explanations for the drop in crime rates that made up the "conventional wisdom" about crime rates but "only three can be shown to have contributed to the drop in crime." (p 121). The same is happening in the current Social Security financial crisis. The solution to the crisis is not fully focused on the main cause of the crisis. The main reason crime rates went down according to Freakonomics is that there were fewer "potential criminals" to become "actual criminals." This idea is reflected in the basic question in Freakonomics: where have all the criminals gone?

> In the early 1990s, just as the first cohort of children born after Roe v. Wade was hitting its late teens – the years during which young men enter their criminal prime – the rate of crime began to fall. What this cohort was missing, of course, were the children who stood the greatest chance of becoming criminals. (p139)

It is what this "first cohort of children born after Roe v. Wade" was missing that is the key to how abortion affects the social security financial crisis and why perhaps solutions do not focus on stopping abortion as the main cause. In the crime rate situation what was missing was the cohort of "children who stood the greatest chance of becoming criminals." Logically it also would be missing several other "cohorts" of adults including those important to the System's revenue. In fact the first post Roe v. Wade cohort of teenagers and adults was missing "all the adults" who would have been born in the 1970s had they not been aborted. It was missing criminals and mothers who most likely would have given birth to more criminals according to Freakonomics had these "cohorts" not been aborted. Logically among the "other cohorts" eliminated by abortion from the "general" post Roe v. Wade cohort would be those who represent the System's future revenue base – covered workers.

> It wasn't gun control or a strong economy or new police strategies that finally blunted the American crime wave. It was, among other factors, the reality that the pool of potential criminals had dramatically shrunk (p 6)

Similarly it was not declining fertility rates, the surge in baby boom retirees, declining labor force participation rates or other factors that caused the growth rate in the covered worker cohort to diminish. It was, similar to crime rates in Freakonomics, the reality that the pool of potential covered workers had dramatically shrunk. The argument that the pool of actual criminals went down because the pool of potential criminals went down is an application of the Principle of Potentiality/Actuality and explains how abortion affects the pool of actual covered workers as well as the pool of actual criminals.

What a substance is really or actually right now is its actuality—for instance, I am sitting on an actual chair. Yet, what a substance has the prospect to become is its potentiality—for instance, an actual boy is a potential adult. http://www.catholicapologetics. info/catholicteaching/philosophy/cause.htm

Obviously an adult at one point in its development was an actual boy with the potential to become an adult. Likewise at one point the actual boy was a fetus with the potential of becoming a child and then an adult person. An unborn person has the potential of becoming an adult person. Some adults commit crimes and some become productive members of the work force.

The idea that analogical reasoning would be an effective way of demonstrating the validity of the abortion/covered worker theory is based essentially on another key idea in Freakonomics that scientific discovery is a matter of knowing what data to look for and how to measure it. Often it is a matter of looking underneath what appears to be happening in pursuit of answers to some "odd and perhaps frivolous questions" to discover what really is happening.

What this book is about is stripping a layer or two from the surface of modern life and seeing what is happening underneath…We will seek out the answers in the data…often we will take advantage of patterns in the data that were incidentally left behind…(p12)

One of those questions obviously was how is the theory in Freakonomics evidence that the theory developed in this book also is scientifically valid. Logically, what was really "happening" with respect to all those abortions in the 70s and 80s would show up in the cohorts that drive social outcomes including crime but other outcomes as well some 20 years later.

The "cohort" analysis also is one of the stronger pieces of evidence of similarity between the two theories. Like the "criminal pool," the "covered worker pool" is one of these cohorts affected by abortion. The effect of abortion on this particular cohort not only had a similar time lag and similarly also had remained hidden but how it was manifested was essentially hidden also. One of the reasons for its not being apparent in the covered worker pool is the fact that the affect of abortion was manifested in a "growth rate" and growth rates are not something terribly transparent. In fact "underneath the data reflecting absolute growth" in covered workers was the fact that the effect of abortion on crime rates and the social security system's revenue base would be reflected in "growth rates" of the two and not so much in "absolute" growth of the two. The absolute size of the System's revenue base could and did increase. However the increase each year was less and the growth rates were less.

Proof of the validity of the abortion/crime rate theory, arguably, was based on analogical reasoning as well as statistical analysis. However the theory in this book uses only analogical reasoning. The fact that it is based on its similarity with a theory based on empirical data using statistical analysis is considered empirical evidence and not simply pure logic. The methods are highly similar. Both theories make extensive use of logical arguments that explain how to a large extent elements of nature "actually work."

The scientific method of measurement in Freakonomics was a combination of correlation analysis and, arguably, analogical reasoning. Correlation analysis determined the probability that abortion was the main cause of the drop in crime rates.

One factor to look for would be the correlation between each state's abortion rate and its crime rate. Sure enough the states with the highest abortion rates in the 1970s experienced the greatest crime drops in the 1990s, while states with low abortion rates experienced smaller crime drops. (This correlation exists even controlling for a variety of factors that influence crime a state's level of incarceration, number of police, and its economic situation.) (p 141)

To explain why the pool of criminals would shrink authors of the abortion/crime rate theory introduced a concept called "unwantedness" and, arguably, used analogical reasoning to explain why potential criminals would become actual criminals. As indicated above the reasoning also reflects an application of the Potentiality/Actuality Principle.

In other words the very factors that drove millions of American women to have an abortion also seemed to predict that their children had they been born would have led unhappy and possibly criminal lives. (p139)

"Unwantedness" according to Freakonomics is a function of the woman's "environmental" circumstances. Typically she has little income, is relatively uneducated and is or would be a single parent. A child born into the same environment – a single parent, with low income and relatively uneducated - stood a good chance of becoming a criminal. The logical conclusion of this line of reasoning, according to Freakonomics, is that a child in this circumstance is unwanted and "unwantedness" was a cause, perhaps a main cause, of crime. Logically by aborting a child in this circumstance reduced the pool of criminals and crime rates. The logic according to Freakonomics was that legalized abortion caused less "unwantedness" and less "unwantedness" caused less crime.

The basic method of reasoning connecting crime rates to unwantedness, arguably, is reasoning by analogy and is the method used in this book to prove the truth of the abortion/covered worker theory. The argument in Freakonomics that unwantedness leads to less crime, arguably, is based on the similarities between the abortion situation in Romania and several Eastern European and Scandinavian countries and the abortion situation in America in the 1990s relative to the influence of environmental factors on criminal behavior. The general conclusion of the studies of the situation in these countries was that unwanted children – those who were not aborted - had a good chance of becoming criminals.

> The children born in the wake of the abortion ban (in Romania) were much more likely to become criminals than children born earlier. (p 136). Studies in other parts of Eastern Europe and in Scandinavia found a similar trend. In most of these cases, abortion was not forbidden outright, but women had to receive permission from a judge in order to have one. Researchers found that in instances where women were denied an abortion she often resented her baby and failed to provide it with a good home. Even when controlling for the income, age, education, and health of the mother, the researchers found that these children too were more likely to become criminals.

The similarity between the Romanian/Eastern European/Scandinavian situations, arguably, is based on the fact that abortion was banned in most states in the U.S. up until the late 1960s as it was in the countries mentioned. Women in the U.S., according to the discussion in Freakonomics, who were denied an abortion, faced essentially the same situation women in Romania, Eastern European Counties and Scandinavia faced who were denied an abortion. The logic is reasoning by analogy.

> The Supreme Court (in Roe v. Wade) gave voice to what the mothers in Romania and Scandinavia – and elsewhere – had long known: when a woman does not want a child she usually has good reason. (p 138).

The Supreme Court in Roe v. Wade also essentially declared that the unborn child had no rights including a right to life. If the child was unwanted it could be destroyed. The statement in Freakonomics in which the "unwantedness" theory is expressed taken as a whole indicates that crime rates fell because the pool of criminals to commit crimes was less because legalized abortion gave women who did not "want" a child a lawful opportunity to destroy the child when it was a potential criminal. Roe v. Wade did not change the moral law.

> Perhaps the most dramatic effect of legalized abortion, however, and one that would take years to reveal itself, was its impact on crime. In the early 1990s, just as the first cohort of children born after Roe v. Wade was hitting its late teen years….the crime rate began to fall. What this cohort was missing, of course, were the children who stood the greatest chance of becoming criminals. And the crime rate continued to fall as an entire generation came of age minus children whose mothers had not wanted to bring a child into the world. Legalized abortion led to less unwantedness; unwantedness leads to high crime; legalized abortion, therefore, led to less crime (p139).

The similarity between criminals and covered workers also is made obvious by the above statement. Both criminals and covered workers have the same "potentiality" by "nature" as unborn children as any unborn child naturally has. All unborn children have the potential to become criminals and members of any other cohort of the population including covered workers. It is how nature works. Logically abortion reduced the pool of potential covered workers that resulted in a declining growth rate in the pool of actual covered workers.

The concept of unwantedness has important implications for the abortion/covered worker theory. Unwantedness, arguably, is similar to the concept of "inconvenience" that often is given as a reason for aborting a child. An unwanted fetus is an inconvenience. An inconvenient fetus is, at least potentially, an unwanted fetus. Most of the reasons listed (in Freakonomics p 138) for why a woman may choose abortion can be grouped under the general category of "inconvenience." An unwanted child logically is one that might be imagined to be disruptive, troublesome, bothersome, or bad timing etc. These reasons are not necessarily related to the mother's income, marital status or level of educational. Logically abortion in many cases is a function of "inconvenience" which perhaps is a type of "unwantedness." It could be argued that abortion destroys "inconvenience" in the same way it destroys unwantedness. It removes the thing that is causing the inconvenience. Legalized abortion, according to Freakonomics reasoning, lowered the price of abortion making abortion more accessible to low income women and easier to get rid of their unwanted child (unwantedness). In the same respect abortion reduces "inconvenience." Legalized abortion gives a woman an opportunity to get rid of the "person" causing the inconvenience. In fact one of the effects of abortion apparently was to give some women a new form of birth control.

> Conceptions rose by nearly 30 percent, but births actually fell by six percent, indicating that many women were using abortion as a method of birth control...(p 139)

As evidence that abortion would logically affect the covered worker pool there is evidence that abortion most likely also reduced the pool of potential covered workers by destroying children who otherwise would have wound up in middle to upper class traditional family situations. One of the effects of abortion, according to Freakonomics, was a dramatic fall in the "number of babies put up for adoption "which has led to the boom in the adoption of foreign babies." (p139). Most of the individuals were not low income, relatively uneducated single persons. They were couples looking for children to adopt. And not finding them in the U.S. caused them to look overseas because the pool of children available for adoption has shrunk.

> The demand for healthy babies is extremely high among American and European parents, who are willing to spend upwards of $25,000 to $50,000 in fees and travel costs. That kind of money — multiplied many thousands of times over — has led to cases of corruption in many countries. http://www.npr.org/2011/11/17/142344354/fewer-babies-available-for-adoption-by-u-s-parents

Logically "unwantedness" can explain why potential criminals might become actual criminals but it is not dissimilar to "inconvenience." Logically many of the aborted children would have wound up in homes where they were wanted and would have become productive citizens including members of the covered worker force.

Studies show that the educational, income level and quality of neighborhood are factors in determining the behavior of persons in later life. In fact, the evidence seems to indicate that, arguably, there is more "wantedness" than "unwantedness" in the world when it comes to life after birth. Children may not be as inconvenient as some people believe. They also may be very convenient when they are needed later in the mother's life.

The fact that "potentially" productive persons can become "actual" productive persons is illustrated in the lives of many public figures. Perhaps one of the more outstanding is the life of the founder of one of the top corporations in America. Stephen Jobs is an example of a child (not a fetus) "unwanted by his parents" most likely because of the "inconvenience" factor (his parents were graduate students at a major University) but "wanted" by his adopted parents. Jobs seemed to have "replicated" his adopted father's productive inclinations not his birth father's.

> As an infant, Steven was adopted by Clara and Paul Jobs and named Steven Paul Jobs. Clara worked as an accountant, and Paul was a Coast Guard veteran and machinist. The family lived in Mountain View, California, within the area that would later become known as Silicon Valley. As a boy, Jobs and his father would work on electronics in the family garage. Paul would show his son how to take apart and reconstruct electronics, a hobby that instilled confidence, tenacity and mechanical prowess in young Jobs. http://www.biography.com/people/steve-jobs-9354805#early-life

The life of Jobs supports the logical conclusion that many children had they not been aborted most likely would have become covered workers. The life of Jobs indicates that not all children whose biological parents did not want them grow up to become criminals. It indicates also that many abortions are explained by the "inconvenience" factor rather than adverse economic factors and that even "unwanted" children can grow up to become productive members of society trough the replication effects. Logically abortions in the 1970s through the 1980s have had a significant impact on the covered work pool today and will have in future years as both the time lag and replication effects become real.

Data relative to labor force participation rate and the percentage of jobs covered by social security indicate, in fact, that well over half and perhaps as many as three-fifths of the potential covered workers most likely would have been productive members of the covered worker population had they not been aborted. The labor force participation rate indicates the percentage of persons born who become members of the labor force. It is estimated to be about 63 percent of the total population. Almost 90 percent of the jobs in the U.S. are covered by social security called covered employment. People in covered employment contribute to the Social Security System. It is natural that persons would want and need to work. It is not only logical but a matter of fact that more than half of them would wind up in covered employment.

For purposes of comparing the abortion/covered worker theory with the abortion/crime rate theory the logical arguments of each is expressed using syllogistic analysis. A syllogism is a type of "logical argument" that bases the truth of its conclusion on the truth of the premises upon which it is based. If the premises of the argument are true the conclusion is true. There are three parts or propositions to a syllogism: a major premise, minor premise and conclusion. The first statement is the "major premise" and the second is the "minor premise." The subject of the minor premise must be the subject of the conclusion. The predicate of the major premise must be the predicate of the conclusion. Obviously for the conclusion (the third statement) to be true both premises must be true based on objective evidence. The premises cannot be "assumed" to be true. If one premise is false the conclusion is false.

The statement in Freakonomics that: "legalized abortion led to less unwantedness; unwantedness leads to high crime; legalized abortion therefore led to less crime" (p 139) expressed in syllogistic form with the first statement as the major premise; the second the minor premise and the third the conclusion appears as follows:

> Legalized abortion led to less unwantedness
> Unwantedness leads to high crime
> Legalized abortion leads to less crime.

This syllogism as stated is not considered in valid syllogism form. For a valid syllogism the subject term of the conclusion (legalized abortion) must be the subject term of the minor premise. Likewise the predicate term of the conclusion (less crime) must be the predicate term of the major premise. Also if "unwantedness leads to high crime" then logically the more there is unwantedness the higher crime will be. Conversely, less unwantedness leads to the lower crime. The second statement expressed in words with equivalent meaning must be the major premise for the syllogism to be in standard form. The predicate of the major premise – leads to less crime – is the predicate of the conclusion. In order to make it a valid syllogism the order of the statements are changed without changing the conclusion. The abortion/crime rate theory in syllogistic form is:

> Less unwantedness leads to less crime.
> Legalized abortion leads to less unwantedness.
> Legalized abortion leads to less crime.

The two premise statements have been rearranged but their meaning and their validity is not changed. The two premises are still true based on the evidence from Freakonomics and the conclusion is the same and true. The conclusion statement is based on the theory in Freakonomics and is based on statistical analysis. The two premises, however, both major and minor premise, arguably, are based on analogical reasoning.

The abortion/crime rate theory also can be expressed in a syllogism using potential criminals as a substitute for crime. Freakonomics notes the connection between potential criminals and actual criminals (p 6). When authors of Freakonomics suggest that 1.5 million abortions might translate into 15,000 human lives they are asserting, arguably, that abortion destroys human lives (see the discussion on p 144). Logically a person has to be a potential criminal before he/she can become an actual criminal. Thus the idea that abortion destroyed potential criminals before they become actual criminals is a likely explanation for why crime drops. The truth of the premise that aborted children are unwanted children is self evident. A syllogism using these terms requires that potential criminals be the predicate term of the conclusion and that aborted children are the subject. It is true both empirically and self-evident that aborted human persons are unwanted human persons. It also is true based on data from Freakonomics and the Principle of Potentiality/Actuality that all unborn human persons have the potential of becoming criminals. The changes in terms are consistent with statement in Freakonomics.

> All unwanted children were potential criminals
> All aborted children were unwanted children.
> All aborted children were potential criminals.

The truth of both the major and minor premise is both self-evident and based on the theory in Freakonomics as well as logical reasoning. The abortion/covered worker theory expressed in the same syllogistic form as the abortion/crime rate theory with only the predicate term of the conclusion changed shows why the two theories are highly similar and how abortion and the social security crisis are linked:

> All unwanted (fetuses) children are potential covered workers.
> All aborted (fetuses) children were unwanted (fetuses) children.
> All aborted (fetuses) children were potential covered workers.

In the syllogism for the abortion/covered worker theory the truth of both the major and minor premises are logically self evident and data from Freakonomics.

These similarities demonstrated by syllogisms are the basis of the conclusion that the inference that abortion most likely is the main cause of the diminishing growth rate in the covered worker pool is essentially the same as the inference in Freakonomics that abortion is the main cause of the drop in crime rates. The major premise (first premise) in the abortion/covered worker theory is essentially the same or at least dramatically similar to the major premise in the abortion/crime rate theory in Freakonomics. The truth of the minor premise (also similar to the minor premise of the abortion/crime rate theory) is self evident but also is based on the theory in Freakonomics. A rational woman would have to not want a child in order to abort the child. Her unwantedness may be forced but unwanted nevertheless. Aborted children are (were) unwanted children. Thus, the syllogism is valid and the conclusion considered reasonable, entailed in the premises and true. The conclusion is analogous to the conclusion reached in Freakonomics.

A test of the truth of the abortion/covered worker theory that abortion most likely is the main cause of the decreasing growth rate in covered workers are in the data reflecting what is happening to the System's revenue base. The data and analysis that follow are intended to demonstrate the consistency of the theory with what it predicts.

There are a number of measures that reflect this consistency. However perhaps the most important is what is happening to the growth rate in the System's revenue base and its total revenue. Between the 1990s and 2000s the average number of covered workers for the decade increased by about 17 million (see Table 2-1). However the "growth rate" dropped by over one-third – from 1.4 percent to .9 percent. The growth rate during the 2000s was a little over half of what it was in the 1980s. Most likely it was the 23 million abortions in the 1970s and 1980s that was the main cause of the drop in growth rates in the 1990s and 2000s.

An analysis of data relative to covered workers (the System's revenue base) indicates why these trends may have gone unnoticed. The "pool of covered workers" has increased every year. However the growth rate in the average number of workers for each decade has decreased since the 1970s. And this happens to be the problem for the Social Security system: revenue is growing at a lesser rate than expenses.

Table 2-1

Growth Rates of Average Covered Workers for the Decade
By Decade

Decades		Average Worker Pool (000)	Average Growth Rate
1970s		101,314	2.0%
1980s		119,635	1.7%
1990s		140,367	1.4%
2000s**		157,073	0.9%
2000s***		157,509	0.3%
** through 2007			
*** through 2010			

Source: Calculations by author based on data from Trustees 2012
Report.

The growth in the System's revenue and expenses reflect the same
trend. Total revenue (including non-tax revenue) has been declining
since the 1980s (Table 2-2). In fact the growth rate in the decade of
the 2000s was less than half (43 percent) of what it was in the decade
of the 1980s.

Table 2-2

Growth Rates in the Social Security
System's Revenue and Expenses
By Decade

Decade			Revenue	Expense
1980s			10.3%	7.5%
1990s			5.9%	5.0%
2000s			4.5%	6.5%
2000 % of				

Source: Calculations by author based on data from Trustees 2012
Report.

By contrast the growth rate in expenses during the same time span has declined by only about one-seventh (15 percent) of what it was in the 1980s – 7.5 percent compared to 6.5 percent. There most likely is a natural reason why the growth rate in expenses would not match the growth rate in revenue. The "time lag" between abortion and its effect on the benefit population is much longer than its affect on the covered worker population. People enter the labor force about 20 years after they are born. They don't retire until about 65 years after birth. The time lag is about 45 years longer.

There are several other measures of the financial solvency condition of the Social Security system that are commonly used that support the inference of this theory. An analysis using each of these measures all point to the same conclusion – that abortion most likely is the main cause of changes in the System's revenue base and its revenue.

The dependency ratio discussed above is one of the more commonly used measures. This ratio measures the number of covered workers in relation to the number of beneficiaries. The dependency ratio remained above three until the System began experiencing operating deficits in 2010. After 2010 based on projections by Trustees of the System the ratio will decline reflecting the slower growth in covered workers compared to the growth in beneficiaries (Table 2-3).

Table 2-3
Dependency Ratio – 2009 to 2037 Projected

Year	Covered Workers*	OASIDI Beneficiaries*	Dependency Ratio
2009	156,021	51,860	3.0
2010	155,170	53,494	2.9
2012	157,883	55,102	2.9
2015	168,734	61,533	2.7
2020	175,961	69,863	2.5
2025	180,105	78,185	2.3
2030	184,128	84,952	2.2
2035	188,600	89,754	2.1
2037	190,540	91,084	2.1

* Data and Projections by Trustees

By 2037 the ratio will have declined to about 2 to 1. It is this situation that causes Trustees of the System to warn that what amounts to an "abortion tax" will be necessary to maintain financial solvency.

The projections for calculating the dependency ratio in Table 2-3 are projections by Trustees of the System for covered workers and beneficiaries through 2090 based on the Trustee's "assumptions" for the "intermediate" range of projections. Projections based on the "intermediate" projections (used in this analysis) indicate the long term nature of the forces leading to the crisis reflected in the declining "dependency ratio." The dependency ratio in 2011 was about 3:1. By 2035 it is projected to be about 2:1. By 2090 it is projected to be a little less than 2:1. However the projections are based on the assumption that the fertility rate will decline from a little over two in 2010 to about two by 2035 and then remain at two through 2090. However there is no apparent assumption about the behavior of abortions.

A statement by Trustees of the System reflects the sensitivity to the System's financial solvency to factors such as the fertility rate to which abortion is highly similar. Both a lower fertility rate and an increase in or constant level of abortions results in fewer human persons being born. The effect of a falling fertility rate has the same effect on the covered worker population as abortion. In fact the situation as reported in Freakonomics reflects the affects of abortion rather than a lower fertility rate. In the period after Roe v. Wade conceptions went up 30 percent but live births went down six percent.

The "fertility rate" is a key factor in economic growth and an indication of how abortion affects the economy and the Social Security System. For example the fertility rate was about 3.7 in the 1950s (the middle of the baby boom years) but had dropped to about 1.7 by the mid 1980s. Economic growth during the 1970s and 1980s – about 20 years after the baby boom years – was the fastest and longest in the history of the U.S. economy. The economy in the 2000s has experienced slower growth. Most likely much of the economy's slower growth performance is explained by the one million abortions each year since the 1970s and 1980s. Likewise economic problems associated with slow economic growth are logically related to the abortion rate some 20 years ago.

Fertility rate assumption used by Trustees in their projections is considered the key to projections of covered workers and a reflection of what could happen if the fertility rate were lower. For the fertility rate to remain essentially at its current level – about two – the trend over the past several decades would need to somewhat reverse itself. The current fertility rate (about 2.08) is slightly below the replacement rate (about 2.11). The Trustee's high cost projections based on a fertility rate assumption of 1.7 reflect the problem if it falls below two. A fertility rate of 1.7 would cause the dependency ratio to drop to 1.4 to 1. If a fertility rate of two requires a 25 percent cut in benefits a fertility rate of 1.4 would require an even deeper cut. Most people probably would consider a larger "abortion tax" to sustain financial stability as outrageous! A fertility rate of 1.7 is in fact larger than the fertility rates in many European countries and Japan and Russia all having serious economic problems.

Trustees of the System apparently recognize that a declining rate of live births will have an impact on the solvency of the System as reflected in the lower dependency ratio but apparently assume that the change to a lower dependency ratio is explained significantly by a decline in the fertility rate. The "demographic shift" as it is referred to by Trustees is reflected in the fertility rate assumption by Trustees of the System but the statement is somewhat problematic. In the report on the <u>Financial Status of the Social Security Program</u> in the section entitled "What is causing the financial status to show shortfall?" Trustees of the System recognize that the fertility rate dropped by about one-third between the baby boom years but has remained at about two since 1965.

> Birth rates that averaged over three children per woman during the baby boom period (1946–1965) dropped to just two children per woman by 1970 and have remained at about that level since that time (see Chart 10). ...After 1965, however, the total fertility rate shifted to a new level around two children per woman. It is this apparently permanent shift to lower birth rates in the United States that is the principal cause of our changing age distribution between 2010 and 2030 and the resulting shift in the ratio of beneficiaries to workers. http://www.ssa.gov/policy/docs/ssb/v70n3/v70n3p111.html

Data and discussion from Freakonomics, arguably, demonstrates that abortion more than likely explains more of the System financial crisis than fertility rates.

> In the first year after Roe v. Wade …(abortion) representing one abortion for every 4 live births. By 1980 the number of abortions reached 1.6 million (one for every 2.25 live births where it leveled off (p 138).

Data in Table 2-4 support the conclusion that abortion explains more of the declining growth in the covered worker population than fertility rates. Theoretically at a fertility rate of about 2.1 that is considered the "replacement rate" the population would remain stable. It would not grow nor decrease. Likewise and generally the covered worker population would not grow or decrease unless other factors change. In the 2012 Trustees Report in the section entitled "Long Range Demographic Assumptions…" the chart showing historical fertility rates indicates the trend in fertility rates since the 1970s. The rate dropped in 1980 from 2.4 in 1970 but increased to near the replacement rate in 1990 and 2000. On the other hand the number of abortions almost doubled between 1973 and 1980 and doubled between 1973 and 1990 and remained at a more than double the number in 1973 through the 2000s. Likewise the abortion rate showed the same trend. The rate in 1973 was about four times the rate in 1970. It almost doubled between 1973 and 1980 and 1990 and has remained more than five times the rate in 1970 through 2000. The number of abortions and the abortion rate data are from a report entitled U.S. Abortion Rates, 1960 – 2013 at http://www.johnstonsarchive.net/policy/abortion/graphusabrate.html

Table 2-4

The Abortion Rate, Number of Abortions and Fertility Rate
For Select Years from 1970 to 2010

Year		Abortion Rate [1]	Abortions (millions)	Fertility Rate
1970		4.5	n/a	2.43
1973		16.3	0.7	n/a
1980		29.3	1.3	1.82
1990		27.4	1.4	2.07
2000		21.3	1.6	2.05
2010		17.7	1.1	1.95
2011		17	n/a	2.03

[1] Per 1,000 women age 15 to 44.

A decrease in the fertility rate generally has the same affect on population growth and in turn the growth in covered workers as an increase in the abortion rate. If one is not changing or changing very little (fertility rate at the replace rate) and the other is high compared to the 1970 rate (abortion rate high) and the trend in the covered worker population reflects a decreasing growth rate the trend logically would be affected only slightly if at all by changes in the fertility rate but significantly by changes in the abortion rate. The fertility rate was about 15 percent less in 1980 than it was in 1970 indicating a drop in the covered worker population. However the 1990 fertility rate increased about 14 percent over the 1980 rate what would theoretically cause an increase in the covered worker population. At the same time the abortion rate decreased somewhat after 1980 but remained more than five to six times what it was in 1970. Since a high abortion rate has the same effect as a low fertility rate these data indicate that the effect of the "demographic shift" (as Trustees call it) after 1980 is more likely due to the abortion rate than the fertility rate. Logically the high abortion rate after 1970 explains more of the change in the covered worker population since 1980 than changes in the fertility rate.

The financial crisis situation of the System is reflected in a measure of solvency called the Trust Fund Ratio. This ratio indicates the problem the system will face when reserves are gone (2037) (See Table 2-5). The trust fund ratio measures the financial resources at the beginning of the year to pay expenses for that year. Financial resources to pay expenses include current revenue plus the systems reserves. A positive ratio indicates solvency. A negative trust fund ratio reflects financial problems. A value of 0 for the ratio indicates no reserves and a dependency on current revenue to meet current obligations. The reality is the trend in this measure also points toward financial crisis. The trust fund ratio began declining in 2010 and will reach zero by 2037 when the reserves are gone and the abortion tax or some other drastic action will be required to maintain solvency.

Table 2-5
Trust Fund Ratio compared to Dependency Ratio
Actual and Projected

Year	Covered Workers*	OASIDI Beneficiaries*	Dependency Ratio	Trust Fund Ratios
2009	156,021	51,860	3.0	353
2010	155,170	53,494	2.9	357
2012	157,883	55,102	2.9	340
2015	168,734	61,533	2.7	302
2020	175,961	69,863	2.5	240
2025	180,105	78,185	2.3	164
2030	184,128	84,952	2.2	70
2035	188,600	89,754	2.1	0
2037	190,540	91,084	2.1	0

* Data and Projections by Trustees

Source: Trustees 2012 Report.

A Trust Fund Ratio of 0 in 2037 coincides with a dependency ratio of 2 to 1 in 2037. According to Trustees of the System solvency depends on the System's ability to pay scheduled benefits. A negative

Trust Fund Ratio indicates potential insolvency. A zero value indicates that unless revenue is equal to scheduled benefits the later cannot be paid.

> Solvency at any point in time requires that sufficient financial resources are available to pay all scheduled benefits at that time. Solvency is generally indicated by a positive trust fund ratio. "Sustainable solvency" for the financing of the program under a specified set of assumptions has been achieved when the program has positive projected trust fund ratios throughout the 75-year projection period that are either stable or rising at the end of the period. http://www.ssa.gov/oact/tr/2012/IV_B_LRest.html#455750. (see third paragraph under B. Long-Range Estimates.)

As indicated in Table 2-5 the trust fund ratio reaches 0 by 2035 at which point the dependency ratio is 2 to 1. One of the assumptions considered necessary for financial solvency is the assumption that the "natural dependency ratio" as it was referred to above is in fact 3 to 1 if benefits are to be paid at the 100 percent level. Otherwise financial solvency is achieved by assuming that benefits will be cut.

The revenue rate and the cost rate that affect the trust fund ratio include items that somewhat hide the main cause of the problem. The revenue rate includes sources of revenue that essentially are temporary. For example if general fund transfers include the transfer of assets held as reserves mostly in the form of U.S. Government securities then these transfers stop when reserves are exhausted. If these are the reserves then they are projected to be exhausted by 2037. When these are gone the only way to finance expenses is from current tax revenue.

The annual income rate is the ratio of all non-interest income to the OASDI taxable payroll for the year. Non-interest income includes payroll taxes, taxes on scheduled benefits, and any general fund transfers or reimbursements. The OASDI taxable payroll consists of the total earnings subject to OASDI taxes with some relatively small adjustments.[1] The annual cost rate is the ratio of the cost of the program to the taxable payroll for the year. The cost includes scheduled benefits, administrative expenses, net interchange with the Railroad Retirement program, and payments for vocational rehabilitation services for disabled beneficiaries. For any year, the income rate minus the cost rate is the "balance" for the year. (see first paragraph under B 1 of Long-Range Estimates at http://www.ssa.gov/oact/tr/2012/IV_B_LRest.html#455750

The cost rate includes items that are much less temporary and therefore more difficult to deal with. Administrative expenses especially and vocational rehabilitation expenses probably will be much more difficult to shed.

It should be obvious that the abortion tax will force many older and disabled Americans to look elsewhere than the Social Security System for survival after 2037. The tragedy is there may be nowhere else to look. The idea of the replication effect is significant both on individuals and on society. Not only is abortion a significant threat to a viable "public" security system it is a significant threat to a "private" security system as well. Logically among the other adult cohorts that abortion destroys are the potential caregivers for elderly and disabled parents and grandparents that would have become actual caregivers had they not been aborted. Not only does abortion destroy potential criminals and potential parents and grandparents it destroys whatever these persons would have become in their adult years. Abortion also destroys children and grandchildren with the potential of providing financial security and care for parents and grandparents in their retirement years. Abortion destroys the "private" economic security system.

The basic propositions arguably contained in the abortion/crime rate theory in Freakonomics are considered highly pertinent for the abortion/covered worker theory in this book. This writer's understanding of these key propositions includes:

- The unborn child is a human person with potential.
- An unborn child with potential can become a criminal when he/she becomes an adult.
- Abortion causes the pool of human persons with potential to shrink (get smaller).
- The situation of the mother is a determinant in her child's becoming a criminal.
- There is a multi-generation (replication) effect to abortion.
- An aborted fetus is an unwanted fetus.
- All aborted children were unwanted children.
- All aborted children were potential criminals as well as something other than criminals.
- All aborted children were potential covered workers and caregivers.

In the abortion/covered worker theory these propositions become:

- All unborn children (fetuses) have potential.
- All unborn children have the potential to become a covered worker in the social security system when he/she becomes an adult.

- All abortions cause the pool of human persons with potential to become covered workers and/or caregivers to shrink (get smaller).
- The situation of the mother is a determinant in her child's becoming a covered worker.
- Abortion eliminates not one but several generations of potential covered workers.

These propositions that are or support the premises of the abortion/crime rate theory are the support for premises in the abortion/covered worker theory stated above and restated in syllogistic format:

All unwanted children are potential covered workers.
All aborted children were unwanted children.
All aborted children were potential covered workers.

The similarities between the abortion/crime rate theory in Freakonomics and the abortion/covered worker theory in this book are strong and comprehensive. Covered workers are known to be similar to criminals in that both are human persons. They both at one time were "human persons (fetuses) with potential." The reason some became criminals according to Freakonomics is most likely explained by their environment as they grew from birth to adulthood. It included their mother's situation at the time she became pregnant because it would be the situation in which the child grew to become an adult. The same logic explains why some would become covered workers. It depends on their mother's situation as they most likely would replicate their parents. The cause in the two theories is the same – abortion. In both cases the specific effect is at least highly similar if not identical - the destruction of human persons with potential. The general effect is a destruction of a condition known to affect the life and quality of life of individuals, families and society. In addition the "time lag" between abortion and the time they became productive or unproductive members of society is about the same – 20 years.

There is similarity also in how the effect of abortion is manifested in each case. A reduction in "crime rates" is similar to a "reduction in the growth rate of covered workers." It cannot be argued that this manifestation is the same in each case because the two measures are calculated differently. However they are similar in that both are manifested in the "declining growth rate" of the "pool" affected by abortion. Arguably it was the "growth rate" in the number of criminals that went down that caused crime rates to go down. Logically for there to be fewer criminals the growth rate would need to be negative which is going down.

The effect abortion has had on the covered worker pool is not insignificant. In fact it is substantial as the analysis in the following chapter will show.

Abortion and the Lost Covered Workers

Why Abortion is the Main Cause of the Abortion Tax

When a tragedy strikes a nation one of the first logical questions is: how many lives were lost? A similar question with respect to the 50 million abortions over the past 40 years is: how many covered workers were lost? The reality is that abortions in the past 40 years and those in the next few years by 2037 will cause a "gap" between the number of covered workers "required" for financial solvency and the "actual" number as projected by Trustees of the System. The inference is that abortion most likely is the main cause of this disparity. Logically to be the main cause of the crisis abortion would need to explain most of the disparity.

This disparity is referred to in this book as the "covered worker gap." The way the U.S. Social Security pay-as-you-go system is structured if there are 50 million beneficiaries then 150 million covered workers are required for the System to remain financially solvent and sound and pay benefits at the 100 percent level. A dependency ratio significantly below 3 to 1 signals financial trouble.

The 3 to 1 ratio is considered the "required" or "natural" dependency ratio for financial solvency.

One of the many insights about abortion gained from Freakonomics is the insight that the effect of abortion depends on who gets aborted – male or female. One of the affects of abortion and one that will have an impact on the covered worker gap is a phenomenon discussed in Freakonomics called the "replication effect."

> And the post-Roe cohort was not only missing thousands of young male criminals but also thousands of single, teenage mothers—for many of the aborted baby girls would have been the children most likely to replicate their own mothers' tendencies (p 141).

The replication effect of abortion is another of the "hidden" effects of abortion that has significant implications for the Social Security solvency crisis. If the person aborted is a female then the impact of a single abortion is greater than if the person aborted is a male. An aborted female eliminates not just one potential person but several. Females become mothers who have daughters who tend to duplicate or "replicate" what their mothers did. Among other things they have children. The idea of the replication effect is that aborting a female who happens to have children who grow up to become criminals destroys not only one woman but the daughter and granddaughter, etc, that would have been born plus the children they would have had if the first woman had not been aborted who likely would have had children who had the potential of becoming criminals when they became adults. The replication effect of abortion is a reality of abortion. The tragedy of the replication effect of abortion with respect to the covered worker population is that abortion eliminates not just one generation of workers but several.

The replication effect also is evidence of how abortion actually affects social outcomes. In order for a post-Roe cohort to be missing actual mothers it had to be missing potential mothers. Abortion eliminates potential human persons who, in the case of the replication effect, would have become "...single, teenage mothers."

What all this leads to is the logical conclusion that the magnitude of the effect of abortion on the covered worker pool is greater than the 50 million abortions in the past 40 years. From 1973 to 2010 there were about 52 million abortions. Abortions beginning in 1973 eliminated mothers that would have begun having children in 1993. Theoretically about half of the 52 million abortions should have been women who as potential mothers would most likely have "replicated" what their mothers did: have children who also had children. These roughly 26 million aborted women were the potential mothers of about 52 million children about 25 million of whom could have impacted the covered worker pool by 2037. The total effect of abortion since 1973 is summarized in Table 3-1. The projection considers abortions through 2010. The replication effect on the covered worker pool is estimated to be about 14 million.

Table 3-1

Total Abortions, Potential 2nd Generation Abortions and Potential Covered Workers Lost by Abortions up to 2010

Years	Actual Abortions	Potential 2nd Genertion	Total	Potential Covered Workers
1973 to 2010	51,788,497		51,788,497	29,281,216
1993 to 2010		25,426,000	25,426,000	14,375,860
Totals	51,788,497	25,426,000	77,214,497	43,657,077
* Covered worker participation rate:			56.5%	

Source: Calculations by author based on abortion data compiled by Robert Johnston at: http://www.johnstonsarchive.net/policy/abortion/graphusabrate.html

This projection of about 44 million lost "potential covered workers" considers a labor force participation rate of about two-thirds and a covered worker to total employment rate of about 88 percent. That is the basis for the "covered worker participation rate" of 56.5 per cent (88 percent of 66 percent). Every 10 abortions cause the loss to the covered worker pool of almost nine covered workers.

The gap calculation also considers the beneficiary population as projected by Trustees of the System. Since it takes about three covered workers to pay the expense of one beneficiary the required number of covered workers for solvency depends on the number of beneficiaries. At a dependency ratio of 3 to 1 if there are 90 million beneficiaries then about 270 million covered workers are "required" for financial solvency unless benefits are cut.

The dependency ratio of about 2.9 is considered the "natural constraint" and is referred to in this chapter as the "optimum dependency ratio" because it is the one that reflects financial solvency in the System. The actual dependency ratio is the ratio at any particular point in time. The "optimum dependency ratio" does not change as long as the system's structure does not change.

The actual dependency ratio has been falling since the 2000s based on the average number of covered workers and beneficiaries for each decade. It is less in the 2010s (2.7) than it was in 2000s (3.3) and is projected to be less in decade of the 2020s (2.3). It wasn't until 2010 that revenue fell below expenses that operating deficits began and the Trust Fund Ratio began falling reflecting the use of reserves to make up the shortage of revenue. The growth rate in covered workers has been diminishing since the 1970s (see table 3-3 below). The average growth rate in the 1980s (about 1.7 percent) was about twice what it was in the 2000s (.9 percent). It was 1.4 percent in the 1990s.

The projections of covered workers and beneficiaries are taken from projections by Trustees of the System. Total beneficiaries include the disabled component. In 1990 this component was about 11 percent of total beneficiaries. In 2000 and 2010 respectively it was about 16 percent and 19 percent respectively. By 2037 the disability component is projected to be about 14 percent of total beneficiaries and is projected to grow at the same rate as retirees for the 2037 to 2085 period. There is no doubt that some of the financial stress on the System has been caused by growth in the disability component during the 2000s. Regardless it is the growth rate in the covered worker pool that represents the real problem for the U.S. Social Security system especially by 2037 when the benefit cuts (abortion tax) will be necessary.

The "covered worker gap" projection also considers the labor force participation rate; the covered employment rate, age entering the work force and the length of careers and retirements. Assumptions for these key variables are based on analysis of current and historical data. There are no data available that indicate that the assumptions for these key variables will materially change for the projection period.

Projections regarding the replication effect are based on the fertility rate assumption used by Trustees of the System for their intermediate projections. As shown in the 2012 Trustees Report the fertility rate was about 2.07 in 1990 and 1.95 in 2010. For the intermediate projections the rate is projected to fall through 2035 to 2.0 and remain at 2.0 for the next 50 years. The high cost projections (by the Trustees) are based on the assumption that the fertility rate will drop to 1.71 by 2035 and remain at 1.7 for the next 50 years. What happens to the fertility rate will drive substantially what happens to social security and perhaps the whole U.S. Economy. In fact a fertility rate of 1.7 for 50 years most likely would be associated with what has been called the "demographic winter" which would be catastrophic for all Americans not just beneficiaries of the Social Security System.

Based on the assumptions indicated the projected "gap" between the number of workers required for maintaining solvency in the social security system and the actual number is about 74 million covered workers by 2037 (Table 3-2). The "covered worker gap" in 2015 will be about 10 million. A gap begins to appear in 2012 increasing each five year interval from less than two million in 2012 to almost 74 million by 2037.

Table 3-2
Calculation of Covered Worker Gap by Time Period

Year	Covered Workers*	OASIDI Beneficiaries*	Dependency Ratio	Required Covered Workers**	Covered Worker Gap
2009	156,021	51,860	3.0	150,394	(5,627)
2010	155,170	53,494	2.9	155,133	(37)
2012	157,883	55,102	2.9	159,795	1,912
2015	168,734	61,533	2.7	178,446	9,712
2020	175,961	69,863	2.5	202,603	26,642
2025	180,105	78,185	2.3	226,737	46,632
2030	184,128	84,952	2.2	246,361	62,233
2035	188,600	89,754	2.1	260,287	71,687
2037	190,540	91,084	2.1	264,144	73,604
* Data and Projections by Trustees					
** Based on dependency ratio of 2.9					

The growth rate problem is reflected in the data in Table 3-3. The growth rate in the covered worker population has been declining from the 1970s through the 2000s while the growth rate in beneficiaries has remained essentially constant through the 1980s, 1990s and 2000s. A two percent growth in covered workers in the 2000s would amount to about three million workers. The growth rate in covered workers by the 2000s through 2007 had dropped to about one-half of what it was in the 1970s (2.0 to .9). The growth rate in the 2000s was a negative 45 percent from what it was in the 1980s.

Table 3-3
Growth in Covered Worker Population

Decades	Average Worker Pool (000)	Covered Workers		Beneficiaries	
		Average Growth Rate	Change in Growth Rate****	Average Growth Rate	Change in Growth Rate
1970s	101,314	2.0%	n/a	3.6%	n/a
1980s	119,635	1.7%	n/a	1.2%	n/a
1990s	140,367	1.4%	-16.3%	1.3%	15.0%
2000s**	157,073	0.9%	-45.4%	1.4%	21.0%
2000s***	157,509	0.3%	-82.3%	1.7%	47.8%

** through 2007
*** through 2010
**** measured from 1980

The basic problem the system is facing is reflected in the <u>growth rate</u> of covered workers and not the <u>absolute</u> number of covered workers. Actually the absolute number of covered workers has increased during this entire period. However the increase each decade has been at a "diminishing rate." The number increased by about 21 million between the 1980s and 1990s but only 17 million the next decade (between the 1990s and 2000s.) Most likely the growth in covered workers during the decades of the 1970s and 1980s reflect the low abortion rate in the baby boom years of 1946 to 1964 and the higher fertility rate. The growth rates in the 1990s and 2000s reflect the lower fertility rates in the 1970s and 1980s (perhaps as much as one-third lower) and more significantly the surge in abortions in the 1980s and 1990s. Abortions in the 1980s were more than double what they were in the 1970s. Most likely the decline in the growth rate of covered workers in the 2000s is related to the high abortion rate in the 1980s and 1990s.

The real problem of the U.S. Social Security system can easily go unnoticed if one is not familiar with the dependency ratio and its key determinants. <u>As long as the "growth rate" of covered workers is less than the "growth rate" of beneficiaries as has been the case for several years the System will eventually and inevitably encounter financial disaster.</u>

The growth rate in beneficiaries reported in Table 3-3 began to increase slightly in the 2000s due partly to the growth in the disability component while the decline in the growth rate of covered workers declined even more (from 1.4 to .3 percent). The baby boom generation probably did not contribute to this disparity as baby boomers did not begin to retire until 2011. Unless one "looks underneath the data" (as Freakonomics would say) to what is happening to "growth rates" the connection between fertility rates and abortions in the 1980s and 1990s and the declining growth rate in the covered worker pool but not the beneficiary pool could go unnoticed.

The data indicate that the problem is substantially a problem in the diminishing growth rate in the system's revenue base causing a shortage of revenue and the financial difficulties the system faces. As long as this situation continues the abortion tax will be necessary.

The data in Table 3-4 summarize projections of what is called the "lost covered workers" and is an estimate of the effect abortions from 1973 to 2017 most likely will have on the covered worker pool by 2037. The estimated number of generations between the years 1973 and 2037 is 2.5 and one generation between 2012 and 2037. An abortion in 1973 would eliminate a child (about 1993) and a grandchild in (2013). Potentially the one abortion in 1973 eliminates the potential of 2.5 potential persons assuming a fertility rate of two and half the children are female.

The effect of abortions between 1973 and 2017 is the loss of about 56 million potential covered workers. The estimated number of abortions during this time frame is 59 million. Based on the replication effect this 59 million eliminated another 35 million children and five million grandchildren.

Table 3-4

Total and Actual Potential Covered Workers Lost
To Abortion between 1973 and 2017

Years of Abortion	Years of Employment	Actual Persons	Potential Abortions		Lost Potential Workers [1]
			Children	G Children	
1973-2010	1993-2035	51,788,497			29,281,216
2011-2017	2035-2037	7,232,895			4,089,479
1993-2017	2013-2037		35,537,550		20,092,931
2013-2017	2033-2037			5,173,400	2,925,040
Total		59,021,393	35,537,550	5,173,400	56,388,667

Assumptions:
* Average participation rate (70s .64; 80s .61; 90s .65; 00s .67) = 64.3%
* Percent employment covered by social security 88.0%
    Covered worker participation rate (CWPR = 64.3% x 88.0%) 56.5%
* Individuals enter work force at age 20 and work for 45 years.
* Women begin having children at age 20.
* Average fertility rates for decade of 80s -3.5; 90s- 3.0; 00s-2.9
* Woman aborted in 1973 would potentially have had children (3.5)
    in 1993 and grandchildren (2.9) in 2013 assuming half are female.
[1] Total abortions (actual+children+gchildren) x CWPR

Source: Calculations by author based on abortion data compiled by Robert Johnston at: http://www.johnstonsarchive.net/policy/abortion/graphusabrate.html

The gap between the required and actual number of covered workers reflected in Table 3-5 indicates that abortion most likely is the main cause of the destruction of 56 million covered workers of the 74 million gap by 2037. Abortion explains about three-quarters of the gap of 74 million covered workers. The data in Table 3-5 is similar to the data in Table 3-2 except that the effect of the lost covered workers has been added.

Table 3-5

Calculation of Lost Covered Worker Potential by Time Intervals
2009 to 2037
(000)

Year	Covered Workers*	OASIDI Beneficiaries*	Dependency Ratio	Required Covered Workers**	Covered Worker Gap	Lost Covered Workers	Lost as Percent of Gap
2009	156,021	51,860	3.0	150,394	(5,627)		
2010	155,170	53,494	2.9	155,133	(37)		
2012	157,883	55,102	2.9	159,795	1,912	16,120	842.9%
2015	168,734	61,533	2.7	178,446	9,712	20,062	206.6%
2020	175,961	69,863	2.5	202,603	26,642	27,827	104.4%
2025	180,105	78,185	2.3	226,737	46,632	35,837	76.9%
2030	184,128	84,952	2.2	246,361	62,233	43,657	70.2%
2035	188,600	89,754	2.1	260,287	71,687	52,308	73.0%
2037	190,540	91,084	2.1	264,144	73,604	56,389	76.6%

* Data and Projections by Trustees
** Based on dependency ratio of 2.9

Beginning in about 2025 abortions that have already occurred will account for more than three-fourths of the shortage in covered workers needed to maintain financial solvency in the System. The 52 million abortions that already have occurred will result in the loss of about 36 million covered workers – almost 77 percent of the 47 million covered workers needed to maintain solvency in the system.

The basic conclusion of the abortion/covered worker theory is that abortion is considered the main cause of the social security financial crisis and the abortion tax. This is so because abortions appear to be the cause of about three-fourths of the gap between the number of covered workers "required" for financial solvency and the "actual" number. No other single factor and even all other factors combined could not explain more. The analysis has demonstrated that abortion explains a large percentage of the covered worker gap and accordingly is most likely the main cause of the crisis.

There remains two issues that must be addressed in order for the abortion/covered worker theory to have the effect that it is hoped it will have. Both have to do with the morality of abortion. One issue has to do with whether or not the "morality" argument of the abortion industry is based on sound reasoning or faulty logic. The other is whether the tactics of the abortion industry to attract clients are consistent with basic moral precepts including the Golden Rule precept. In the spirit of Freakonomics an honest assessment of these issues will provide perhaps new insights into why what is happening is happening and new insight into perhaps why the "abortion tax" is as tragic as it is. The morality argument of the abortion industry and the morality of tactics used by the abortion industry are analyzed in the following two chapters.

The Morality of Abortion

(It doesn't work the way some would like it to work)

Morality is not about how some would like it to work. However 50 million abortions in the past 40 years would seem to indicate that many people think it does. Given that morality actually is about our situation in life after death (eternal happiness or eternal suffering depending on what we did to each other during our earthly lives) this situation led to the freakish idea that there seems to be a gross misunderstanding about how morality actually works especially when it comes to abortion.

The approach to the morality issue here is not so much about how morality actually works. Rather it is more about how one can be "tricked" into thinking it works the way some (those doing the tricky logic) would like it to work. There are numerous scholarly articles available about how morality actually works and how the morality of abortion actually works. Perhaps what is needed is a discussion on how morality does not work because there are arguments (by the abortion industry) that are based on how one would like it to work and not on how it actually works. And these arguments are a major source of confusion.

The discussion in Freakonomics that, arguably, suggests that morality logically works the same way economics works and since economics works according to objective, universal laws grounded in the Natural Law morality most likely works the same way.

> Morality, it could be argued, represents the way that people would like it to work—whereas economics represents how it actually does work. (p 13).

It could be argued that morality represents personal preference and people made rules but the reality is there are objective universal laws governing moral behavior just as there are objective universal laws governing economic behavior. And it seems obvious that a world view that includes the idea that "dramatic effects often have distant, even subtle, causes" (Freakonomics, p 13) spoken in the context of Norma McCorvey (the woman in the Roe v. Wade Supreme Court decision legalizing abortion) was at least alluding to the fact that like economics the effects of abortion when it comes to morality may be "dramatic, distant, and even subtle."

How morality actually works is defined in Natural Law theory just as how economics actually works is defined in economic theory. The theory detailed in earlier chapters of this book defines how abortion is the main cause of the Social Security financial crisis. But since the cause of the crisis is abortion and abortion is a morally charged issue then how the morality of abortion is understood is critical to solving the crisis. It must be understood that not only is abortion destroying the Social Security System but the root cause of the tragic outcome for millions of older and disabled Americans is illogical thinking about the morality of abortion. How morality is understood appears to be inconsistent with how it should be understood, which from a freakish perspective, most likely is the root cause of why there is a Social Security financial crisis in the first place.

Much of the public's misunderstanding about morality most likely is caused by the abortion industry itself and perhaps intentionally so. Generally the arguments of abortion advocates are based on a mistaken and illogical belief that "the end justifies the means." The way morality actually works in order for an action like abortion to be morally good not only must the "end" be good but the "means" and the "intention" must be good also. If anyone of the three is evil the action itself (abortion in this case) is evil. In fact as defined in Freakonomcs (p 144) the "right to choose" argument boils down to the fact that the "right to chose abortion trumps any other factor." Since most of the reasons for elective abortion boil down to convenience then the right to convenience, according to the abortion industry's argument (if there is such a thing) trumps the unborn child's right to life. Based on this type of morality the end (convenience) justifies the means (killing the fetus). An argument that abortion trumps any other factor not only is befuddling but the persons making the argument have not proven it to be a sound argument.

For an argument to be sound (true) the premises upon which the argument is based must be objectively true meaning they cannot be assumed to be true. They must be consistent with the basic moral precepts found in the Divine Natural Law and Scripture.

A detailed discussion of the various foci and "schools of Natural Law" is outside the scope of this writing and the expertise of this writer. For such a discussion the reader is invited to consider an article by Russell Hittinger and a discussion of the article by a number of theologians in the same source. The article is entitled: Natural Law and Catholic Moral Theology at: http://www.scotthahn.com/

download/attachment/3796. The article discusses three foci of Natural Law Theory. Of the three foci, the one based on God's mind is considered the foci that really matters when it comes to issues such as good and evil and life after death.

> Discourse about natural law can gravitate toward any one or a combination of these three foci: law in the human mind; in nature; and in the mind of God., The theologian is (or ought to be) concerned with the third of these three foci; namely natural law as an expression of divine providence. (Hittinger, p2).

The article discusses and explains that the Divine Natural Law is "written by God in the hearts of man" and is essentially how God thinks on the matter. Man's conscience which, according to the article, is where God planted His Natural Law is as much a part of man's human nature as his physical organs. In fact man can know "what he must do to gain eternal happiness" if he is capable of sound reasoning and his reasoning follows his "rightly informed" conscience. Man intuitively knows that unjust killing is wrong. If he thinks logically he should be able to "reason" that abortion amounts to unjust killing.

A morality based on how "some would like it to work" obviously is a "man-made" morality. In order for a "man-made" law to be valid it must be consistent with Divine Natural Law. This basic precept is embedded in the Declaration of Independence when the founding fathers and mothers recognized that there were certain "inalienable rights" endowed by the creator and off limits for government manipulation. When it comes to morality it is the Divine Natural Law that counts.

There are several aspects of the morality issue about which the public could be confused. However there is one highly important aspect of the morality issue that is not necessarily befuddling but could lead to an individual making a bad decision about abortion if it is not a part of one's morality thinking. It must be understood that there are consequences to immoral behavior just as there are consequences to violating any law. Generally when people unknowingly or intentionally violate the law it is because they do not understand the penalty (consequences) or they risk the penalty thinking risking consequences is worth whatever is the gain. It can be an illogical case of the end justifying the means type thinking. People may behave immorally if they think the consequences of their behavior do not matter much and the monetary or convenience they gain seems worth the risk. There may be consequences but they can be minimalized to the point that they do not discourage immoral behavior. This situation is similar to the day care situation in Freakonomics (p 23) where the gain in convenience (for being late picking up their child) was worth the penalty (a small monetary fine) for the same reason. The fine they paid eliminated the moral guilt. But this is the problem with the "end justifies the means" type illogical thinking. People still violate the moral law which is what counts when it comes judgment time. The consequence for violating the laws of morality is eternal punishment in life after death and it is not a trivial matter. The consequences are hell and they last a long time and it is illogical to think otherwise.

The basic argument of the abortion industry (considered the right to choose argument) is framed in legal rights but not basic moral precepts or natural rights. In fact no comparison is made between the two rights which is much of why there is confusion on the matter. Since many are somewhat befuddled by the distinction between legal rights and natural rights the abortion industry's "talking points" justifying abortion capitalizes on the situation and tends to befuddle many into supporting abortion who otherwise may not support abortion if they understood how rights actually works. This is considered especially true when one considers that the U.S. Social Security System may be a casualty of this type of thinking – illogical moral thinking.

The freakish approach to the situation involves looking underneath the abortion industry's argument to the premises to determine whether the argument is valid or invalid. A syllogistic reasoning approach is used to isolate the facts, logic or assumptions upon which the conclusion is based. It approaches the argument of the abortion industry philosophically as a logical argument and not as a religious interpretation of scripture. In logical argument, if the argument is a sound argument, the conclusion is true and the premises upon which the argument is based are true objectively and not subjectively. A "premise" is a statement upon which a conclusion is based. However for a conclusion based on the premise to be true the premise must be true. Consider the following argument:

1. All free men have natural rights
2. Jon is a free man
3. Jon has natural rights

The argument has three statements. The statement "Jon is a free man" is a premise. It says something about Jon and Jon is the subject of the conclusion. The first statement also is a premise – it says something about free men. The third is the conclusion. The conclusion (Jon has natural rights) flows from the premises. The conclusion is true because the premises are true. They also are based on Natural Law theory. Both premises also are self-evident truths. Reason indicates their truthfulness.

Consider the following invalid argument:

1. All free men have the natural right to unjustly harm their neighbor
2. Jon is a free man
3. Jon has the natural right to unjustly harm his neighbor

The conclusion (Jon has the natural right to unjustly harm his neighbor) is an invalid argument – it is not true. It is not true because one of the two premises – the first (called the major premise) is not true. It is in fact contrary to Natural Law. In order for the argument to be true both premises have to be true. Again the major premise (first statement) is not true because it is inconsistent with the Natural Law which is known in this case by reason. That it is not true is self evident.

An advantage of the syllogistic analysis approach is that is makes transparent what must be true in order for the argument to be true. To be true a premise of an argument must be based on factual evidence or on sound logical reasoning following the rules for sound argument and by a creditable source (person or persons other than the individual making the argument). The proof of validity can be creditable science research or it can be creditable philosophical research and teaching. It can also be self-evident – something commonly experienced by most people. If the individual making the argument assumes the premise is true without proving it is true it is said that he/she is "begging the question." He/she assumes to be true what they conclude is true. Such an argument is illogical thinking.

In a natural law approach the truth of the premises are based on their consistency with basic moral precepts found in Natural Law theory. The analysis of the morality arguments seeks to achieve objectivity by following the approach to the morality issue taken by authors of Freakonomics. Arguably Freakonomics looked at the logical soundness of the argument from an economic perspective using what in economics are called opportunity cost and spillover cost techniques of analysis. An economic approach is a logical approach. The method in this chapter is highly similar. It is a logical approach but from a Natural Law perspective. The Natural Law approach looks at what are considered the basic premises of the morality argument of the abortion industry in terms of their consistency with sound moral reasoning which basically is a matter of looking at them from the standpoint of objective moral standards. Actually what authors of Freakonomics found using an opportunity cost approach (trade-off analysis), arguably, is that abortion is bad economics. It looked like there may be an "unintended benefit" to abortion (it lowers crime) but the opportunity cost analysis concluded otherwise.

The basic precept of the moral law according to St. Thomas Aquinas is "do good and avoid evil." Thus the basic task is to demonstrate that the arguments of abortion proponents are inconsistent with this "do good and avoid evil" precept and other basic precepts of the moral law (justice and truth) in order to demonstrate why they are illogical and misleading. The basic argument considered to be an attempt at a morality argument by the abortion industry is the right to choose argument. To assure objectivity in the analysis in this chapter the analysis is based on the argument as it was defined in Freakonomics. The right to choose argument is the argument that "the right to choose abortion trumps any other factor" (Freakonomics p 144). The object is abortion. As is pointed out in Freakonomics the argument assumes that abortion "trumps" any other factor.

In this regard it is assumed that for a moral precept to be objectively sound it must be found in both the Divine Natural Law and Scripture. It must be consistent with standards of how morality actually works and how it should work. Since both Scripture and the Divine Natural Law are authored ultimately by God then it follows that moral precepts found in "both" are what is in God's mind. Natural Moral Law and any interpretation must be based on sound reasoning of a consensus of qualified philosophers and theologians whose job it is to interpret and explain the natural law which basically is how the Natural Law and Scripture came to be. Basically these sources confirm the legitimacy of the Divine Natural Law and Scripture as sources of sound moral precepts.

> According to natural law moral theory, the moral standards that govern human behavior are, in some sense, objectively derived from the nature of human beings and the nature of the world. http://www.iep.utm.edu/natlaw/
> Morality is the distinction between right and wrong. It is the determination of what should be done and what should not be done. Morals deal with behaviors as well as motives. There is a great deal of discussion on what is the source of morals and whether or not they are objective. Biblically, morals are derived from God's character and revealed to us through the Scriptures. https://carm.org/dictionary-morality

There essentially are only two basic moral precepts that really matter when it comes to the morality of the abortion issue. These two are justice and truth and the two are inextricably related. According to the teachings of St. Thomas Aquinas justice requires truth as "Other virtues annexed to justice include *truthfulness*, since the just person will always present himself to others without pretext or falsehood" (http://www.iep.utm.edu/aq-moral/#SH3d) section 3 on Justice. Justice requires that the unborn child's rights be protected and not violated. The precept of truth requires that those seeking information about abortion including its morality be given information based on empirical evidence or sound argument or both.

An enlightening discussion of the topics including the Natural Law and Natural Rights thinking is contained in an article by John S. Baker entitled Natural Law and Justice Thomas at http://www. regent.edu/acad/schlaw/student_life/studentorgs/lawreview/docs/ issues/v12n2/12RegentULRev471.pdf

In a paper entitled "The Moral Philosophy of St. Thomas Aquinas" presented at the Thomistic Conference Vilnius, Lithuania July 2000, Kenneth W. Kemp Department of Philosophy University of St. Thomas St. Paul, Minnesota, USA, explains St. Thomas' Natural Law teaching and the linkage between Natural Law and Objective morality. When Kemp asks the rhetorical question: "But is not St. Thomas' doctrine of the existence of a natural law at the very center of his moral philosophy?" it is understood by this writer that, arguably, Kemp's answer clarifies any doubt about the linkage between Thomas's Natural Law and Objective morality (p 13).

> This view gains what currency it has from the casual identification of St. Thomas' doctrine of a natural law with the Objectivity of Morals Thesis. Perhaps there is an historical connection between the term "natural law" and the idea of the objectivity of morals. The term seems to have emerged from the observation that, to put it in modern dress, the details of what it takes to make a contract valid varies somewhat from one jurisdiction to another, but the principle that contracts should be honored is common to all jurisdictions. Public insults may be criminal in one jurisdiction and not in another, but homicide is a crime everywhere. The variable might be thought of

as conventional law; the common as "natural" law, grounded in universal moral norms. The existence of these common principles is suggested by St. Paul, in his Epistle to the Romans: http://courseweb.stthomas.edu/kwkemp/Papers/MPSTA.pdf

The moral precepts that count, at least when it comes to life after death, are those precepts "common to all jurisdictions." The law legalizing abortion is a "conventional law." But killing (homicide) is a crime everywhere. It is assumed that in "the right to choose an abortion trumps any other factor" any other factor includes the idea of "all" other factors. Any other factor would include Natural Rights which are endowed or inalienable rights. However, implicit in this definition of the right to choose argument is the "thinking" that the right to choose to kill another human person "trumps" the other person's rights including his/her right to life, liberty and the pursuit of happiness. All other factors would include these fundamental rights. The argument assumes that a "legal right" trumps a "natural right." This implies also that civil laws take precedence over and/or can cancel natural laws. This issue is analyzed below.

The relationship between natural and man-made rights is included in the classical form of natural rights theory as taught by St. Thomas Aquinas. One of the basic principles of natural rights theory is that a government cannot abuse the natural rights of people. This writer's understanding of the Natural Law is based in part on the discussion at http://www.encyclopedia.com/topic/natural_rights.aspx. An unjust killing may not be murder (a legal concept) but it is still immoral. A human law or civil law that violates Natural Law is an unjust law. In the section entitled "Unjust Human Law" in an article discussing St. Thomas's Classical Natural Law Theory an example is given specifically regarding abortion. http://home.wlu.edu/~mahonj/PhilLawLecture1NatLaw.htm

Laws can be unjust if, e.g., they require, or even permit, murder. Here they are contradicting Natural Law. For example, it has been argued that legally enforced abortions in China for women with unauthorized second pregnancies are unjust according to Natural Law.

Civil laws or human made laws when they are just themselves are natural and are justified by and made necessary by Divine Natural Law which requires them to be just laws. Civil laws are necessary according to Natural Law theory for the common good of individuals but man-made laws must be consistent with the Natural Law. If they contradict Natural Law then they are essentially no law at all. This point is explained in an article by Thomas D. D'Andrea entitled the Natural Law Theory of Thomas Aquinas. Man made laws are necessary among other things when the precepts of the Natural Law are either beyond human comprehension or are subject to different interpretations by different individuals.

Because of this inherent limitation of the human mind, humans must make their own laws to supplement that portion of the Eternal Law that they do spontaneously and readily grasp (which portion includes the rudimentary parts of the natural law) [15], to direct themselves in community to their fulfillment. They do this correctly either by deriving specific norms from the most basic and general principles or precepts of the natural law, or when they give specific shape to one of these basic and discovered dictates or principles appropriate for a particular time and place Any human law, though, that directly contravenes a dictate of the natural law *ipso facto* fails as a law and has the status of an irrational command instead. Such commands ought to only be observed for prudential reasons, such as to avoid some greater harm that might arise in the social order from the failure to observe what is really only a pseudo-law. (see The Natural Law Theory of Thomas Aquinas by Thomas D. D'Andrea – the last paragraph at http://www.nlnrac.org/classical/aquinas).

A pseudo-law is a law that is false and/or misleading. It would not be binding on human persons the truth of which should be discernible by diligent reasoning by human persons seeking the truth and validity of a matter.

This basic Natural Rights principle that civil laws must be consistent with Natural Law also is embedded in the Declaration of Independence drafted by Thomas Jefferson. Jefferson and the signers of the Declaration considered the right to life an "inalienable right" and not subject to cancelation or change by man-made law.

> Natural and legal rights are two types of rights. Legal rights are those bestowed onto a person by a given legal system. Natural rights are those not contingent upon the laws, customs, or beliefs of any particular culture or government and therefore universal and inalienable (i.e., cannot be sold, transferred, or removed). http://en.wikipedia.org/wiki/Natural_and_legal_rights

This supremacy of Natural Law over laws made by men also is reflected in Martin Luther King's letter from the Birmingham Jail:

> A just law is a man made code that squares with the moral law or the law of God. An unjust law is a code that is out of harmony with the moral law.

> To put it in the terms of St. Thomas Aquinas: An unjust law is a human law that is not rooted in eternal law and natural law." http://en.wikipedia.org/wiki/Man-made_law

What all this discussion and these ideas boil down to is the obvious truth that the right to an abortion and to perform abortions is a legal right and not a Natural or inalienable right. The reality is that the moral consequences of doing and participating in immoral actions are not avoided by thinking or believing they can be avoided by conventional man-made law.

It also is true that the right to life not only is a natural right but also is considered a primary right not only over rights granted by the government but all other natural rights as well.

> "Natural rights," on the other hand, are the rights that all men possess, because of which they may be obligated to act, or to refrain from acting, in certain ways. According to the teaching developed primarily by Hobbes and Locke, there are many natural rights, but all of them are inferences from one original right, the right that each man has to preserve his life. All other natural rights, like the right to liberty and the right to property, are necessary inferences from the right of self-preservation, or are conceived as implicit in the exercise of that primary right. Similarly, the natural law founded upon natural rights consists of deductions made from the primary right and its implications. The sum of these deductions is the state of civil society. The doctrine of natural rights teaches primarily, then, that all obligation is derived from the right which every man has to preserve

his own life. http://www.encyclopedia.com/topic/natural_rights.aspx

The concept of natural rights logically is the basis for the basic moral precept commonly known as the Golden Rule – do unto others what you would have them do unto you. There sometimes is a "Silver rule" version of the Golden Rule which is "don't do to others what you don't want them to do to you." If you don't want others to take your life "unjustly" then don't take the life of others "unjustly."

Syllogistic reasoning is used to demonstrate that what the various arguments of the abortion industry basically are doing to the unborn child and promoting doing to the unborn child is "what they would not want the unborn child to do to them." Using the positive form of the syllogism as indicated above in order for the right to choose argument to be true both premises of the argument must be true. If either premise is false the conclusion is false or at least does not flow from the premises. Proof can be in the form of a sound rational argument, scientific evidence or the truth can be self-evident. A premise of the argument cannot be assumed to be true. To assume that a premise is true without evidence that it is true (logical or empirical) then the argument is a form of "begging the question" which is "faulty logic." When faulty logic is used to justify an action it is considered moral posturing. A first step is to determine what the premises of the right to choose argument are.

Arguably, when authors of Freakonomics looked "underneath" the "right to choose" argument what they found, based on this author's understanding of the discussion are three propositions and/or premises that are considered the premises of the "right to choose" argument.

- Legal rights trump natural rights.
- Right to choose an abortion trumps all other factors.
- The fetus is worthless.

All three propositions are analyzed in terms of Natural Rights theory discussed above. Fundamentally the analysis focuses on the relationship between legal rights and natural rights as something worthless, it could be argued, logically has no rights.

Based on Natural Law theory and natural rights discussed above and based on Divine Natural Law and Scripture there is no natural right to abortion. Based on the evidence – Natural Law, Scripture and the Declaration of Independence - it is self-evident that the right to an abortion is a "legal right" but not an inalienable or "natural right." It is considered self-evident that "natural rights" would be included in the premise "all other factors."

When the argument is expressed in the form of a categorical syllogism "abortion rights trump natural rights" is considered the conclusion of the argument as the syllogism demonstrates. The major and the minor premises are defined according to the rules of syllogistic construction. The object of the conclusion "trump natural rights" must be the object of the major premise. The right to choose an abortion must be the subject of the minor premises and the subject of the conclusion. The "invalid" argument in syllogistic form is:

> All legal rights trump all natural rights.
> All rights to choose an abortion are legal rights.
> All rights to choose an abortion trump all natural rights.

The conclusion of the argument is not true and is illogical since the major premise upon which the conclusion rests is not true. In order for the conclusion to be true both premises must be true. The faulty reasoning for this argument is explained above. In order for a legal right to trump natural rights—morally-- it would be necessary for one person's right to kill another person to take precedence over the other person's right to life. It would be necessary for this to have been the creator's (God's) intention which is highly unlikely. God in natural law theory sometimes is referred to as the "first cause" or the creator. However, such a right is not based on Natural Law theory or Scripture.

The problem with the argument that is based on the premise that "legal rights trump natural rights" is that there is no philosophical, theological or scientific basis for the truth of the premise. The premise is <u>assumed</u> to be true which means that the conclusion is <u>assumed</u> to be true. An argument where the premise and the conclusion are assumed to be true but is not based on objective truth (the facts) is a "begging the question" type argument. Otherwise the argument would have to prove that the right to life can be "removed" by a legal right or it would have to prove that abortion is an "inalienable" right or is based on an inalienable right. Although the minor premise in the argument is true the major premise is not true. In order for the conclusion to be valid both premises must be true.

Although the "begging the question" type argument is considered "faulty reasoning" nevertheless it is an argument commonly used and perhaps even necessary when the proponent cannot justify what he/she is doing morally. And it is clear from the syllogistic construction and reasoning that such a conclusion cannot be made following the rules of sound reasoning which requires the premises to be objectively true in order for the conclusion to be true. By "begging the question" the "faulty reasoning" can befuddle the one for whom the argument is directed. Attention can be drawn away from the real issue and the argument never directs the person to the real moral issue which is whether abortion is good or evil. Even more dangerous is the fact that it is a distraction from the consequences of immoral actions. In this case the argument directs the idea to whether abortion is legal or not and not whether it is moral or not. The real issue the abortion industry seeks to avoid is the "morality of whether one person has the natural right to choose to kill another person." Although the latter person is unborn it is a person innocent, non-threatening and defenseless. It is self-evident to most rational thinking individuals that such a killing is evil and that there is no such right to do evil. An argument that intentionally avoids these ideas is intentionally misleading.

However the reality of human nature is such that when one wants to avoid the moral reality of an issue and the truth is an obstacle to one's personal agenda – which usually is money – then "moral posturing" is necessary and can be especially effective in influencing the illogical thinking of others all of which furthers one's personal agenda which unfortunately is money. When a "connection" can be "invented" and made to or linked to a sound moral precept such as rights or health although the "invented right" is not a sound moral precept the argument can be effective. Most people recognize that women like all human persons have natural rights. They also understand that women have legal rights. However the unjust taking of the life of another person is not a natural right although it is a legal right with respect to abortion. Killing an innocent, non-threatening defenseless human person to advance one's own agenda is not a natural right. But by arguing that women have a right to abortion without explaining the difference between legal and natural rights many can be made to believe that it is a natural right as well.

The logical fallacy of the argument that the right to an abortion trumps endowed rights can be demonstrated by syllogistic reasoning. The argument is based on the premise that legal rights can be removed by government while inalienable rights cannot. There are several reliable sources of evidence for the truth of this argument. Natural Law theory and Scripture are the most reliable. The objective truth of the argument also is found in the U.S. Declaration of Independence where the right to life is considered an inalienable right and is not removable by the government. Another is its consistency with the writings of the great philosophers like John Locke that confirm the truth that inalienable rights are not granted by government but are protected by government. The language contained in the definition of legal and endowed rights are used in the premises and are as follows:

> All legal rights are removable
> All rights to abortion are legal rights
> All rights to abortion are removable
>
> All endowed rights are inalienable
> All rights to life are endowed rights
> All rights to life are inalienable

The premises in each of these arguments are true and proven true by reference to the sources indicated – Scripture, the Natural Moral Law, the U.S. Declaration of Independence and writings of the great philosophers like John Locke – and the conclusion in each case is true. The right to life is an inalienable right. The right to choose an abortion is a legal right that violates a natural right.

The third proposition listed above that the "fetus is worthless" is essentially an argument that the fetus has no rights – legal or moral. The argument frequently is made by abortion advocates that the fetus is a "glob of tissue" and not a human person and therefore has no rights and abortion is not killing a human person. The humanness of the fetus has been proven by ultrasound and DNA technology.

Its personhood has been proven by the empirical evidence in Freakonomics that abortion destroys potential human persons some of whom grow up to become criminals. It also is proven on the basis of potentiality from the writings of both medieval philosophers (St. Thomas) and current philosophers (see <u>Who Counts as Persons</u> by John Kavanaugh) in addition to DNA analysis. DNA analysis shows that the DNA of a fetus is human DNA. These proofs along with the abortion/crime rate theory in Freakonomics are considered scientific proof that the fetus is a human person with potential and not a "glob of tissue." It is not worthless.

However with regard to the "fetus is worthless" proposition the problem and confusion and "faulty reasoning" with the argument is that if the argument is accepted then logically there would be no moral consequences in destroying something considered worthless. When authors of Freakonomics analyzed the "worthless" issue it was analyzed from what they considered a frivolous question: what is the value of a "newborn" compared to an "unborn" (Freakonomics p 144). As both are human persons the question effectively was also asking: what is the value of human life in different stages of development? Authors assumed that a "resolute" pro-choice person would not trade a newborn for a fetus in any circumstance. The logical extension of this argument is that the fetus is worthless. This argument (by the abortion industry) if true would mean that the rights of the fetus are not a factor in the abortion decision. It assumes, again without proof, that a woman's right to kill the fetus takes precedence over the fetus's right to life. Arguably something worthless would have no rights and destroying something worthless in most cases would not have moral implication. Again the categorical syllogism can be used to test the validity of the argument. The premises must be derived from the conclusion which is that: all fetuses are worthless.

All potentially adult persons are worthless.

All fetuses are potentially adult persons.
All fetuses are worthless.

The conclusion in this instance is not true because the major premise is not true. Stephen Jobs at one stage in his development was a fetus with the potential of becoming the founder of a large and successful corporation. Stephen Jobs at one stage in his development was a potential adult person. The minor premise is true based on the abortion/crime rate theory in Freakonomics.

To construct a valid syllogism and a valid argument where the conclusion is that all fetuses are worthless it is necessary that both premises be true. It simply is not possible to construct such an argument and syllogism. It is not possible to define a major premise that fits the conclusion of this argument. Some potential adults (fetuses) may become criminals when they grow up as Freakonomics demonstrates and are worthless in that sense. However, some may become doctors, teachers, laborers, etc., and valuable contributors to themselves, to family and to society such that not "all" fetuses are worthless. Some may become worthless when they become adults but many do not.

However a valid argument can be made and a valid syllogism constructed with the conclusion that all fetuses are potentially valuable adults. The term used in Freakonomics was relative value (p 144). However value used in this sense implies exchange value.

All potential adult persons are potentially valuable.
All fetuses are potential adult persons.
All fetuses are potentially valuable.

The argument in Freakonomics, arguably, is that it is after birth that the child learns to be a criminal. He/she is not a criminal at birth.

The unborn child is a potential criminal but not an actual criminal. Rather the argument is that it is the "environment" after the child is born that determines his criminal behavior. It is not determined at conception. At conception, logically, the fetus is potentially valuable.

A fetus is a potential adult person. Proof of the major premise is empirical evidence (Stephen Jobs) and the self evident truth that each of us if we consider ourselves worth something were potentially valuable adult persons when we were fetuses. Also we like some adult persons have the potential of being able to exchange skills for money. Our own experience and the life of Stephen Jobs proves the major premise. The life of Stephen Jobs cannot be used at the same time in the same sense to prove that all potential adult persons are worthless. All adult persons were at one stage in their development potential adult persons. It is not that all will be valuable in this sense but as fetuses all have the potential of being valuable. This argument is based on the scientific evidence found in Freakonomics that a fetus has the potential of becoming a criminal. It is not based on the argument of "Potentiality" although it could be. However, given that only human persons are criminals and that abortion, according to Freakonomics, reduced the pool of criminals, then the fetus had the potential of becoming a worthless or valuable person when he/she is an adult actually.

It is recognized that not all abortions are considered immoral. The so called "double effect" situation is an example. In situations where abortion is a "secondary effect" and the primary intent of a medical procedure is good then abortion is not evil although the fetus is killed. In cases where a procedure is primarily intended to save a woman's life and abortion is a result the abortion is what is called a "double effect" of the procedure. In these instances the threat to the woman's life is a condition other than her pregnancy. Saving a life is good. In double-effect situations the good effect (saving the mother's life) must outweigh the bad effect (killing the fetus) and due diligence is exercised to minimize the harm. In other words all precautions possible to save the fetus must have been taken. The "woman's health" argument is a candidate for this type of fallacy and tricky logic. Abortion is permissible only when the double effect requirement is satisfied.

Elective abortions do not fall into the "double effect" category. The intent in an elective abortion is not to save the mother's life. It is to terminate the pregnancy. Medical procedures to save the mother's life are not considered evil. In the case of elective abortion the intention of the medical procedure is to kill the fetus which is evil. It is a medical procedure that results in the killing of an innocent, non-threatening, defenseless human person and is not consistent with the Natural Law and especially the Golden Rule. The syllogism that follows demonstrates the "illogical thinking" often associated with elective abortion.

> All unnecessary medical procedures that destroy life are good.
> All elective abortions are unnecessary medical procedures that destroy life.
> All elective abortions are good.

The conclusion is not true because the major premise (first proposition) is not true. An unnecessary medical procedure that is an unjust killing of a human person prevents the human person from achieving its ultimate good and is evil according to the teachings of St. Thomas Aquinas.

It has been argued that many supporters of abortion base their support of abortion and, arguably, the right to choose argument on one of three concepts: the "bodily integrity" argument, the not knowing when life begins argument and the argument of not putting personal views on a moral subject into positive law. http://en.wikipedia.org/wiki/Right_to_life] Bodily integrity rights are important and include among other things protection against physical abuse. Although bodily rights probably are grounded in both legal and natural rights to argue on the basis of an assumption that "abortion" is one of them without proving that it is grounded in Natural Law and/or Scripture is "begging the question." Likewise the other two are considered begging the question type arguments as each assumes is true what it attempts to prove is true. There is scientific evidence (DNA) that life begins at conception. Arguing that one should not put his/her personal views into law appears to be a contradiction in this case as not opposing an action amounts to supporting it as legalized abortion is based on personal views of lawmakers not moral law as there is nothing in the Divine Natural Law that supports abortion.

The other two of the three arguments of the abortion industry to justify what they do – the "woman's health" argument and the "war on women" argument - are difficult to express in categorical syllogism form. One problem is that there is no evidence that abortion is a category of health or war although pregnancy is. However there are some instances where an abortion involves woman's health but elective abortion is not one of them. The "double effect" situation mentioned above is an example where it does.

For a procedure like abortion to improve a person's health it has to have one or both of two effects: prevent an illness condition before it happens or cure a condition that already exists. There is no scientific evidence that elective abortion prevents or cures a health condition including a mental health condition. The fact is most of the research on abortion as it relates to the women's health issue seems to address the question of whether abortion causes health problems rather than prevents or cures them. To be a valid argument it is necessary that the two premises upon which it is based must be true. The premises have to do with the nature of "health" and in the case of mental illness whether abortion is a "psychiatric medical procedure" that addresses mental illness.

The argument expressed in categorical syllogism form has as the conclusion: abortion prevents or cures women's health conditions.

> Some psychiatric medical procedures prevent or cure mental illness.
> Abortion is a psychiatric medical procedure.
> Abortion prevents or cures mental illness.

The problem with this argument is the minor premise (the second statement). Abortion is not considered a psychiatric medical procedure. Since the minor premise is false the conclusion is false.

In the case of elective abortion the procedure not only is not considered therapeutic it is not considered necessary.

> Some therapeutic medical procedures prevent or cure women's health conditions.
> All elective abortions are therapeutic medical procedure.
> All elective abortions prevent or cure women's health conditions.

In this syllogism the problem again is the minor premise (the second statement). There is no evidence that elective abortions are therapeutic.

There is evidence, on the other hand, that abortion may be the cause of mental illness not a cure. Although a report published by the American Psychological Association in 2008 concluded there was no underline creditable evidence underline that "a single elective abortion" caused mental illness the report found some evidence to the contrary.

> Task Force concluded that there is no credible evidence that a single elective abortion of an unwanted pregnancy in and of itself causes mental health problems for adult women. The research consistently found that the backgrounds and circumstances of the women who seek abortions vary. The Task Force found some studies that indicate that some women do experience sadness, grief and feelings of loss following an abortion and some experience "clinically significant disorders, including depression and anxiety." The evidence regarding the relative mental health risks associated with multiple abortions is more uncertain.

The underlined words in the above statement were inserted by this author. The APA (American Psychological Association) report noted there were "high quality" and "low quality" studies that were reviewed but does not define either or implies that they follow the "generally accepted" definitions of both.

> Quality research most commonly refers to the scientific process encompassing all aspects of study design; in particular, it pertains to the judgment regarding the match between the methods and questions, selection of subjects, measurement of outcomes, and protection against systematic bias, nonsystematic bias, and inferential error (Boaz & Ashby, 2003; Lohr, 2004; Shavelson & Towne, 2002). http://ktdrr.org/ktlibrary/ articles_pubs/ncddrwork/focus/focus9/Focus9.pdf

There is no indication of what determines either high or low quality in the APA report and whether the criterion is quality research or quality evidence. The report does not indicate how "adult woman" is defined and at what stage the abortion was performed. It is possible at least as a research question that many if not most abortions are by women other than adult women as perhaps as many as one-fifth of the women seeking an abortion are not "adult women." Slightly less than one-fifth (18 percent) of abortions are by teenagers (age 15 to 19) who logically are not adult women. More than half the abortions are by women ages 20 to 24 who may or may not be considered adult women. Also most abortions are first-trimester abortions. Also the results are based on a "single elective abortion." Studies show that in almost half the cases the abortion is not her "first" as the woman has had one or more abortions before. Thus logically the report applies to only half the abortions.

It is not clear in the APA statement what is meant by "no creditable evidence" but use of the term suggests there must have been some evidence indicating a linkage between abortion and mental illness but it was not considered creditable. "Clinically significant disorders including depression and anxiety" are serious disorders and were listed in the 2008 APA report as the findings in some studies.

In an article in the American Psychologist, published in 2009, authors from six leading universities in the U.S. in a follow up report to the 2008 report of the APA found that:

> the most rigorous studies indicated that within the United States, the relative risk of mental health problems among adult women who have a single, legal, first-trimester abortion of an unwanted pregnancy is no greater than the risk among women who deliver an unwanted pregnancy" and "Some women do

> (experience mental health problems), however it is important that women's varied experiences of abortion be recognized, validated and understood." http://www.apa.org/pubs/journals/features/amp-64-9-863.pdf

This report essentially raises the same questions as the previous report. Also it confirms that what appears to be "creditable research" does confirm that "some women do (experience mental health problems) associated with a single, legal, first-trimester abortion." It confirms that there is risk to abortion as defined but "no greater" than the risk associated with carrying the pregnancy to term. Also to use the conclusion of this report as evidence in support of the abortion industry's argument that abortion causes women's health conditions clearly is problematic.

A concern with these reports in light of the finding in Freakonomics that there is a significant "time lag" between abortion and its effects is whether the "time lag" factor was considered in the studies. Also abortion is considered a "traumatic" experience and is capable of producing PTSD after a period of time perhaps years later. In light of the "time lag" factor associated with abortion it would be logical to consider that the mental health effects of abortion may not manifest itself until years later - perhaps 20 years later. The time lag factor did not appear to be a variable considered in the studies.

A report by an organization dedicated to the study of abortion and mental health showed a stronger linkage between abortion and mental illness potentially caused by the abortion.

> A study of the medical records of 56,741 California Medicaid patients revealed that women who had abortions were *160 percent more likely* than delivering

women to be hospitalized for psychiatric treatment in the first 90 days following abortion or delivery. Rates of psychiatric treatment remained significantly higher for at least four years. http://afterabortion. org/2011/abortion-risks-a-list-of-major-psychological-complications-related-to-abortion/

A rate of 160 percent suggests that abortion is more likely to cause mental illness than carrying the pregnancy to term. The effect also seemed serious as the illness (for the woman to which the 160 percent applied) required "hospitalization" for psychiatric treatment.

With regards to the other morality arguments of the abortion industry the "woman's health argument" like the right to choose argument has similar problems with regards to "sound reasoning." There apparently is no "creditable" evidence to support the truth of the premises and therefore the conclusions. The premises and the conclusion of the women's health argument in all cases is assumed and not proven empirically or logically. Like the right to choose argument the woman's health argument is a "begging the question" type argument and tricky logic.

The issue with respect to the "war on women" argument seems to be a logical fallacy called the "hypocrisy fallacy" as well as a "begging the question" type argument. A hypocrisy fallacy occurs if the person making the charge is the one actually doing what he/she is charging the other person of doing. In this case it seems the aggressors are accusing the defenders of being the aggressors. Logically those waging the war on women would be the aggressors - those who harm women and kill children – especially female children. The actions of those who protect woman and children from harm and death would be considered defenders of women's rights and health. For the argument to be true it would be necessary to show reasonable proof that those who oppose abortion killed unborn children and harm woman. At the same time proof would be necessary showing that abortionists do not kill unborn children and harm women. It should be self-evident to most that proving either argument would be virtually impossible. Obviously the argument is a logical fallacy.

One of the analytical insights from Freakonomics is the need to "look underneath the data (and argument) to see what really is happening" to understand and explain something like a financial crisis. The approach fundamentally is an application of "objective reasoning" from a world view perspective of how the real world actually works. Morality is fundamentally about good and evil and about life after death. The question - where will all the abortion providers go after death for eternity – is the question that really matters. The reality is the morality arguments of the abortion industry appear to be based more on "illogical reasoning" rather than "logical." The analysis was not able to find moral precepts in Scripture and the Natural Law that supported the right to choose argument. Attempts to express the argument in syllogistic form disclosed the faulty logic involved. One or more of the premises upon which the argument is based is not true.

The woman's health argument appears inconsistent with medical science in that abortion does not prevent or cure a medical condition. The war on women argument appears to have the parties to the engagement reversed from their normal roles in a war. In fact in all these arguments there is a "begging the question" fallacy as the premises upon which the arguments are based are "assumed" to be true rather than valid empirical evidence. These arguments also amount to moral posturing as there appears to be no evidence that these arguments are based on moral precepts found in Scripture and the Natural Moral Law and thus are not based on sound objective moral standards.

Moral posturing and the use of faulty reasoning (tricky logic) are considered unscrupulous from a morality perspective. The problem from a morality perspective with "begging the question" fallacies in an argument is that the argument can be very effective in the right circumstance. For the same reason moral posturing also can be effective in the right circumstance. Moral posturing is not something those engaged in a business based on "sound moral precept" do. In reality logical fallacies including begging the question and moral posturing should fall short of providing moral justification for something immoral and usually they do. There remains the final question related to the morality issue: are the tactics used by abortion providers to attract clients unscrupulous as well? This question is explored in the following chapter.

How Abortion Providers attract Clients

Using Information Advantage and Invented Incentive

Unraveling puzzles according to Freakonomics is a matter of asking the right questions. From a freakish point of view one of the not so frivolous questions is why do women have abortions in the first place? Notwithstanding the effects of the moral posturing and begging the question type arguments of the abortion industry having an abortion still seems highly illogical. There are serious health risks – physical and mental – to abortion. Economically it is terribly inefficient as Freakonomics concluded and there are serious moral risks according to Natural Law theory. On the other hand carrying a pregnancy to term logically and practically does not carry any of these risks. So why do women have abortions?

The answer: many if not most are misled! A young woman faced with an unexpected pregnancy is vulnerable to making a bad decision for two basic reasons both discussed in Freakonomics. The biggest problem she has is an information problem. Most likely the young woman has very little understanding about how abortion actually works. She needs to be educated. Secondly most likely her ability to lean and think rationally are impaired by her emotional situation. She is emotionally distraught - a condition that can easily cause her to fear the wrong thing. Under these circumstances the young woman is highly vulnerable to the tactics of an unscrupulous operator. There is a good chance that if she receives misleading information she may do something she otherwise might not do if she had sound information.

What most sound thinking people do when they are faced with a serious medical problem is seek "relevant" information from one he/she assumes is an expert. The abortion provider should have the relevant understanding about how abortion actually works. It is reasonable to think that he/she is an expert in the matter much like a doctor would be perceived as being an expert in a given medical procedure. Whether his expertise is fact or fiction to the extent he is perceived as such the abortion provider has an information advantage. Whether he takes advantage of his advantage depends upon whether his dominant motivation is economic or moral. If the economic incentive dominates there is a good chance he receives a fee and she receives an abortion. And both most likely have engaged in an immoral activity.

The basic problem young women face when seeking help from an abortion provider is that most likely the provider's agenda (money) is inconsistent with the young woman's agenda which logically is about health but also should include the moral incentive (as defined in Freakonomics p 19) – she wants to do the right thing. If information is power then the abortion provider has power. He has the relevant information the young woman does not have or at least is confused about which is why she is seeking information in the first place. And the abortion provider has the economic incentive to advance his own economic agenda over the client's practical and moral agenda. When the typical woman considering an abortion seeks information from an abortion provider there is a very good chance the information she gets will be tainted.

Generally as Freakonomics discusses unscrupulous operators use unscrupulous tactics to attract clients when what they do is morally tainted. Understanding how these unscrupulous tactics work is important in understanding perhaps why many women have abortions.

Two of these tactics abortion providers most likely use for which the young woman is particularly vulnerable will be referred to in this chapter as information advantage and invented incentive. Information advantage is based on the idea of a very real situation in many exchange situations where the product or service involves technical information. It is a situation called "information asymmetry" as stated in Freakonomics:

> It is common for one party to a transaction to have better information than the other party. In the parlance of economists, such a case is known as information asymmetry. (p 68).

Obviously abortion is one of those situations. The procedure is technical with risks and most people have little or none of the relative information to make an informed decision.

The invented incentive tactics is based on the idea that "fear" often is a powerful motivator and that incentives based on emotion (fear) are fairly easy to invent and are effective in the right circumstance.

> An incentive is simply a means of urging people to do more of a good thing and less of a bad thing. But most incentives don't come about organically. Someone— an economist or a politician or a parent—must invent them (p 21).

If the abortion provider provides tainted information and if he/ she invents an incentive that has very little chance of happening without disclosing the odds then the chances of the young woman and the public making a sound decision about abortion is substantially compromised. The relevant moral precepts in the circumstance are justice and truth. The young woman in the circumstance has a right to the truth. In order to satisfy the conditions for moral goodness the intent, action and consequence of the action all must be good. If the intent in each case is to make money by getting someone to do something they might not otherwise do then the tainted information and the invented incentive tactics are most likely immoral. Even though the provider may believe what he is doing is good the fact is taking the life of an innocent, non-threatening defenseless unborn child (the means) is not justified by the end.

The argument that abortion providers use unscrupulous tactics is based on analogical reasoning and not direct evidence. However if they are used there is a good chance the abortion provider is acting immorally and what appears to be the young woman's and public's illogical thinking is explained in part by the tainted information they receive. The immorality of the misuse of information advantage and the use of invented incentives designed to take advantage of the client's vulnerable situation are considered immoral by their inconsistency with basic precepts of morality especially justice and truth. Giving tainted information and taking advantage of the woman's emotional situation is not providing the information to which she is entitled and for which she needs to avoid illogical thinking. The inference that these tactics are used is based on the similarity between situations explained in Freakonomics where disingenuous tactics are known to be used and the typical situation the young woman faces when dealing with an abortion provider. There were "theories" in Freakonomics where school teachers, real estate experts and doctors used "unscrupulous" tactics to attract clients – for a fee. These situations are similar to and can reasonably be applied to the abortion provider. Abortion providers are in the same or highly similar situation as the school teacher that cheats the real estate expert who lies and the doctor who uses invented incentive to persuades his patient to have medical procedures not proven to be effective as explained in Freakonomics (see chapters one and chapter five on the "economics of fear" (p 151). Like the unscrupulous teacher, real estate expert and doctor the abortion provider has an economic incentive to use unscrupulous tactics to advance his own ecnomic agenda – money – over the clients! The provider's client – a young, relatively uneducated, poor and emotionally distraught woman – is highly vulnerable to such disingenuous tactics as she lacks both the relevant information and the ability to think rationally due to her circumstance. For the most part the public is in the same situation.

The situation where information advantage happens is the situation Economists refers to as "information asymmetry." It is a situation where one party to a transaction is in possession of the "relevant information" which the other party lacks. In the case of abortion the relevant information most likely would include information that might make the woman choose an alternative to abortion. Information like health risks – short and long term – and the type of help available she fears losing if she chooses to carry her pregnancy to term is relevant to logical thinking and a sound decision.

The situation where the invented incentive tactic is used is very similar. It is used to take advantage of the woman's emotional condition. One of the more powerful emotions is "fear!" Usually an unexpected and unplanned pregnancy will cause a young unmarried woman to be "emotionally distraught." Emotional distress frequently makes the young woman vulnerable to "false expectations" either those created by her own imagination or those created for her by others including the person from whom she is seeking information – the abortion provider in this case. Having expectations is normal and expectations based on fact, experience or sound logic are natural and can lead to the good consequences intended. However "false expectations" especially those based on fear and created by an "authority figure" can lead to unintended and potentially negative or harmful outcomes as usually happens when the expectations have no factual basis.

> Since children are easily convinced of certain tenets especially when told to them by an authority figure like a parent or teacher, they may believe whatever is taught to them even if what is taught has no factual basis. If the student or child were to act on false information, certain positive or negative unintended consequences could result. http://en.wikipedia. org/wiki /Expectation_(epistemic) #Expectations _impact_on_beliefs

A person who is "emotionally distraught" is highly vulnerable to created "false expectations." False expectations "invented" by the abortion provider based on information that is not factual or is manipulated can cause her thinking to be irrational especially when the false expectation is based on the "fear" of something that is not likely to happen.

> Irrationality is cognition, thinking, talking or acting without inclusion of rationality. It is more specifically described as an action or opinion given through inadequate use of reason, emotional distress, or cognitive deficiency. The term is used, usually pejoratively, to describe thinking and actions that are, or appear to be, less useful, or more illogical than

other more rational alternatives. Irrational behaviors of individuals include maintaining unrealistic expectations, and falling victim to confidence tricks. http://en.wikipedia.org/wiki/Irrationality

False expectations that are wrong are "irrational expectations" because by definition they are not based on truth. Unfortunately false expectations are rather easy to "create" when the potential victim is under emotional distress to begin with. Acting on an "invented" incentive (fear of something not likely to happen) rather than on what she should really fear (something that is likely to happen) leads to illogical thinking and a disastrous decision – morally as well as economically.

The truth is there are long-term consequences of abortion that are truly something real to fear. If they are not considered then the person logically is in the position of "fearing the wrong thing" and a decision based on this situation can be disastrous. What a woman should fear about abortion is the inevitable time in her life when a child would be a significant convenience as for example when she is old, unable to earn income and perhaps disabled. What a person thinking "logically" should fear is the loss of the child when it is urgently needed like when the woman is in her twilight years and cannot provide for herself and has no Social Security benefit.

This is not to deny that carrying a pregnancy to term is not without things to fear. However decisions based on false expectations are not likely to result in goodness – short-term or long-term.

Perhaps the key to understanding why abortion providers would use unscrupulous tactics is in understanding how economic incentive works in the real world. Based on both a common sense understanding of how some would like the world to work (not how it actually works) and on the discussion in Freakonomics it should be self-evident that the incentive to do good frequently is overridden by the incentive to earn money – a fee. According to Freakonomics actions generally are motivated by three types of incentives: social, moral and economic (p 21). The social incentive causes a person to avoid being seen as doing something evil like an older man making a young girl pregnant. The moral incentive is the incentive to do no evil. The economic incentive is about financial reward. Economic incentive is not about others - it is about self!

Economic incentive like everything in nature serves a good purpose when it functions the way nature intended it to function. However according to Freakonomics the reality is (as explained above) there is a "dark side" to economic incentive. It can be more destructive to individuals and society than productive. Crime and abortion are examples. The fact is the economic incentive for the abortion industry is substantial. By any standard abortion is a big business driven by an economic incentive that would thrill almost any entrepreneur – good or bad. The revenue of the abortion industry is estimated to be over $1.0 billion per year. The largest abortion provider performed over 330,000 abortions and performs as much as one-third of all abortions performed. One of the losses resulting from the dark side of economic incentive is the focus of this book: a financially viable social security system. Another is the loss to the woman of a potential care giver in her old age.

The analysis in the remainder of this chapter demonstrates the similarity between situations discussed in Freakonomics where unscrupulous tactics were used and the situation the young woman faces when she seeks advice from an abortion provider.

Logically much of the woman's vulnerability is due to the fact that she most likely views the abortion provider as an expert on abortion.

Like doctors abortion providers provide clients with information the client does not have. Assuming that abortion providers are experts or at least perceived as experts by a woman seeking information about dealing with an unexpected pregnancy then the discussion of experts in Freakonomics explains what she might be up against.

> "Experts depend on the fact that you don't have the information they do. Or that you are so befuddled by the complexity of their operation that you wouldn't know what to do with the information if you had it." (p70)

Information about the abortion procedure also can be "befuddling." Probably to a woman dealing with unexpected pregnancies especially a young, relatively uneducated woman it is befuddling if not explained in fair, lawful and just and complete way. Doctors for example also sometimes depend on the fact that the patient does not have the information the doctor has and for which he makes his money.

> "If your doctor suggests that you have angioplasty - even though some current research suggests that angioplasty often does little to prevent heart attacks- you aren't likely to think that the doctor is using informational advantage to make a few thousand dollars for himself or his buddy." (p 70)

If doctors would use such tactics there is reason to believe abortion providers might use them also.

As discussed earlier one of the most common invented incentives used by persons perceived as experts is based on fear because one of the most powerful motivators happens to be "fear!" It is most commonly used when the client is under "emotional distress" but can be used to motivate the buyer, including a woman considering an abortion, who might otherwise not buy on the basis of logical argument.

> "Armed with information, experts can exert a gigantic, if unspoken, leverage: fear. Fear that your children will find you dead on the bathroom floor of a heart attack if you do not have angioplasty surgery." (p 71)

In many cases the response to fear is rational as in the "fight or flight" response. However when it is the basis for false expectations then the thinking and reaction are considered irrational. As was pointed out in Freakonomics people tend to fear the wrong thing like guns more than swimming pools (p 149). It is considered in this chapter as a type of irrationality. In fact it can be the basis for a tactic called "fear mongering."

> Fear mongering (or scaremongering or scare tactics) is the use of <u>fear</u> to <u>influence</u> the opinions and actions of others towards some specific end. http://en.wikipedia. org/wiki/Fear_mongering

Information advantage can be leveraged by invented incentive and often is used to create false expectations that drive irrational thinking. Emotional stress is one of the situations where fear mongering can be effective.

> "Consider a scenario in which your loved one has just died and now the funeral director – who knows that you know next to nothing about his business and are under emotional duress to boot – steers you to the $7,000 mahogany casket." (p 68)

Fear itself or fear of the inconvenience of the situation appears to be a common theme in the most frequent reasons given for having an abortion.

> Researchers found 40% of these women mentioning something financial, 36% in some way discussing the bad "timing" of the pregnancy, 31% raising a partner issue, 29% speaking of "other children," 20% talking of the child somehow interfering with future opportunities. http://www.lifenews.com/2013/10/10/ why-do-women-have-abortions-new-study-provides- some-answers/

All these conditions can be substantially inconvenient and something to fear. However, at least two of them – the financial and the interference with future opportunities - logically are likely to happen also when the woman is well off financially and when she is older as well as when she is young and not so well off financially. Perhaps they are even more "inconvenient" to the well off older woman than to the younger not so well off woman.

There are several famous and otherwise good thinking women who have experienced a type of fear called the "Bag lady Syndrome" which also is something that can happen in a woman's twilight years including especially women who might have aborted the only child she will or would have had.

> The most documented female money fear is commonly referred to as the "bag lady syndrome," or anxiety about finding yourself suddenly destitute and on skid row. Lily Tomlin, Gloria Steinem, Shirley MacLaine and Katie Couric have all reported suffering from this fear. http://www.forbes.com/2010/09/22/

money-fear-women-forbes-woman-net-worth-finance.html

These logical fears are intended by nature for good reason. However an unscrupulous abortion provider can use them for his "not so good" reason.

From the abortion providers standpoint, the moral precepts most likely violated by misuse of information advantage and invented incentive are the moral precepts of truth and justice. When a person asks for information from one whose services she is considering using he/she has a right to the truth and justice demands that she be given the full and untainted information she needs including truth about the rights of her unborn child in order for her to do "good." Truth according to Mortimer Adler in his book <u>Six Great Ideas</u> generally is the "...conformity of the mind with reality...it regulates our thinking about good." (http://www.thegreatideas.org/apd-trut. html). Manipulating information about a procedure that influences others to make a bad and even immoral decision impairs one's ability to choose good over evil. It is unscrupulous!

The moral precept of justice requires at least that the abortion provider place the woman's agenda on an equal footing as his own. Justice according to St. Thomas Aquinas is the principle that "... denotes a sustained or constant willingness to extend to each person what he or she deserves." http://www.iep.utm.edu/aq-moral/. The woman deserves the truth from one whose services she is considering using. He/she deserves the truth from the expert he/she consults whether a doctor, lawyer or abortion provider. Truth as Adler points out is crucial to how we think and in turn the decision we make in order to do good.

Many women faced with an unexpected pregnancy, especially the first pregnancy, are arguably the type most vulnerable to disingenuous tactics. Based on data from the Guttmacher Institute at http://www.guttmacher.org/pubs/fb_induced_abortion.html as discussed earlier about half the abortions in the U.S. are performed on women age 20 to 24. Slightly less than one-fifth (18 percent) of all abortions in the U.S. are performed on teenagers – ages 15 to 19. Generally persons in these groups—especially the 15 to 19 group--are not well educated; have limited economic means and are not skilled in critical thinking. They are vulnerable to the unsound and unreasonable arguments of one with the information advantage and skill in using fear mongering.

The concern in this instance and perhaps warning is that the effect of and most likely the intention of the abortion provider is to get the client to either ignore or minimize the consequences of abortion as an immoral action. It seems that the abortion provider who uses information advantage and invented incentive tactics himself either ignores the moral reality of the situation or minimizes the consequences. It seems logical that he would get his client to do the same. As discussed in the previous chapter and repeated here there are serious consequences to what some call criminal moral behavior. The analogy used in Scripture is the situation with inheritance. When the rules of the Divine Natural Law are followed (and in the 10 commandments) one is made an "heir" to the Kingdom of God. However doing "evil" according to the first precept of the moral law can cause one to lose his "inheritance." Unfortunately one does not have to know or believe he has an inheritance to lose it.

These ideas and beliefs are generally held among the majority of Americans. A poll by the Gallop Poll organization in 2007 found that "…81 percent said they believe in Heaven; 75 percent in Angels;

and 69 percent in Hell." http://www.christianpost.com/news/ poll-more-americans-believe-in-god-heaven-than-devil-hell-27958/.

Views on the morality of abortion obviously are influenced by Natural Law and biblical teaching. A Pew Research Center poll in 2013 found that slightly less than half (49 Percent) of all Americans believed abortion is immoral. The same poll also found religion to be a factor. About three-fourths of Evangelicals believed abortion to be immoral. Among Catholics there were differences depending upon frequency of attending mass. Among those who regularly attend mass 74 percent considered abortion immoral. The percentage dropped to 40 percent for the so called "lukewarm Catholics" - those who infrequently attended mass. Also the poll found that women are more likely than men to consider abortion immoral. (see the discussion of results at: http://www.prnewswire.com/news-releases/ majorityof-americans-surveyed-believe-heaven-and-hellexist-the-devil-and-angels-are-real-and-god-is-notresponsible-for-recent-us-tragedies-209383941.html.

People also seem to understand how the real world actually works when it comes to good and evil and their relations to life after death. An article entitled "Pew Forum on Religion & Public Life / U.S. Religious Landscape Survey" reported that about three-fourths of the public (74%) believes in life after death. (p 8) and about the same percentage believe in "the existence of heaven (p10). About six in 10 (59%) believe in Hell where "…people who have led bad lives and die without repenting are eternally punished (p 11)." http://www. pewforum.org/files/2008/06/report2religious-landscape-study-key-findings.pdf

While public opinion polls are not a valid basis for moral thinking they help. Notwithstanding the question of the nature of hell it is generally believed by many to be an unbelievably bad condition to be in. It is described as a condition where the "damned" go (along with the demons) after death for their immoral (i.e. evil) deeds and is everlasting. Again notwithstanding the fact that some religions teach that the damned just cease to exist after death (there is no hell) most Americans believe hell is a reality that there is life (existence) after death and its either heaven or hell! There is good reason to believe that there is significant risk in performing abortions and in using unscrupulous tactics to induce others to have an abortion. It would take an irrational thinker to believe that what they are doing is "just" when the best available evidence on the matter (scripture and the natural law) and the majority of Americans apparently believe what they are doing is "unjust!" Blindness to the truth may not be much help in attempts to escape punishment.

Since Hell may be the ultimate punishment for criminal moral behavior it would seem Hell is something to think about. The most authentic source of information about hell is scripture. Since Hell is what one is risking then what Scripture says about it might be worth considering.

> Then I saw a great white throne and him who was seated on it. From his presence earth and sky fled away, and no place was found for them. And I saw the dead, great and small, standing before the throne, and books were opened. Then another book was opened, which is the book of life. And the dead were judged by what was written in the books, according to what they had done. And the sea gave up the dead who were in it, Death and Hades gave up the dead who were in them, and they were judged, each one of them, according to what they had done. Then Death and Hades were thrown into the lake of fire. This is the second death, the lake of fire. And if anyone's

name was not found written in the book of life, he was thrown into the lake of fire. (Revelation 20:11-15 ESV)

Some theologians believe that Hell and the "lake of fire" are two different conditions. One is temporary and one permanent. Most theologians appear to agree that while Hell may be where the damned go before they are finally "judged" by what was written in the "book of life" and that the "lake of fire" is the permanent or final place where the damned go after being judged according to "what they had done" and found unworthy of Heaven.

Whether or not one believes what Scripture has to say on the matter is a matter of faith. However whether it is worthy of belief is matter of reason. Faith is a willingness to accept something as true on the word of another – the bible in this instance. Reason is necessary to determine whether accepting something as true is reasonable. E.g. is scripture a reliable source of God's intention? Faith and reason generally do not contradict each other. However sound reasoning will take any rational person to the fact that Hell is a possibility for life after death! Logically hell is something to fear!

Although most of what we know about hell is based substantially on Scripture and therefore on faith "private revelations" regarding heaven and hell have been reported. There are people who claim to have had a "glimpse of heaven" based on "near death experiences." These NDEs as they are called have been experienced by a range of persons including children (a young as age four) as well as a Harvard trained neurosurgeon. The story of Fatima is different. It was not an NDE and the three children of the Fatima Story claimed they were taken on a tour of hell by the Mother of Jesus. Saint Lucia, one of the three, described what she saw:

"She opened Her (the mother of Jesus) hands once more, as She had done the two previous months. The rays [of light] appeared to penetrate the earth, and we saw, as it were, a vast sea of fire. Plunged in this fire, we saw the demons and the souls [of the damned]. The latter were like transparent burning embers, all blackened or burnished bronze, having human forms. They were floating about in that conflagration, now raised into the air by the flames which issued from within themselves, together with great clouds of smoke. Now they fell back on every side like sparks in huge fires, without weight or equilibrium, amid shrieks and groans of pain and despair, which horrified us and made us tremble with fright (it must have been this sight which caused me to cry out, as people say they heard me). The demons were distinguished [from the souls of the damned] by their terrifying and repellent likeness to frightful and unknown animals, black and transparent like burning coals. That vision only lasted for a moment, thanks to our good Heavenly Mother, Who at the first apparition had promised to take us to Heaven. Without that, I think that we would have died of terror and fear." http://www.fatima.org/essentials/facts/hell.asp

What scripture has to say about hell is no less encouraging. In St. Mark's gospel Jesus himself paints a "terrifying" description of hell when He says: "It is better for you to enter the kingdom of God with one eye than with two eyes to be thrown into hell, where the worm does not die, and the fire is not quenched."

The objective analysis of what abortionist's do and the arguments and tactics they use to attract clients in this chapter seems to demonstrate reasonably that the probability seems high that the abortion industry uses immoral tactics to attract clients. The situations in the various cases in Freakonomics where information advantage and invented incentive were misused were virtually identical to the situations in the real world of abortion. Whether the behavior will result in eternal punishment is a judgment man does not make and no judgment is offered in this writing. However, being blind to the situation does not alter the fact that the risk of an unfavorable judgment seems high. If the assessment is valid then the risk of losing a few dollars by following the precepts of truth and justice is pale compared to the risk of losing Heaven if they are not followed.

The ultimate purpose of the analysis in this chapter is the same as that in the previous chapter which is to prevent the unjust killing of innocent, defenseless non threatening human persons and to save the U.S. Social Security System. Freakonomics has contributed greatly to a better understanding of how the real world actually works and how the abortion industry most likely attracts clients in this case. The situations in the various theories in Freakonomics where these tactics are used by unscrupulous operators are similar if not identical to those found in the abortion industry. When one drills into the issue what one finds is lying and fear mongering to take advantage of uninformed and emotionally distressed young women. Based on Scripture, the Natural Moral Law and common sense the consequences can be severe and eternal and the abortion provider seems vulnerable to both! And millions of older and disabled Americans are vulnerable to losing their economic means of survival.

www.ingramcontent.com/pod-product-compliance
Lightning Source LLC
Chambersburg PA
CBHW030810180526
45163CB00003B/1224